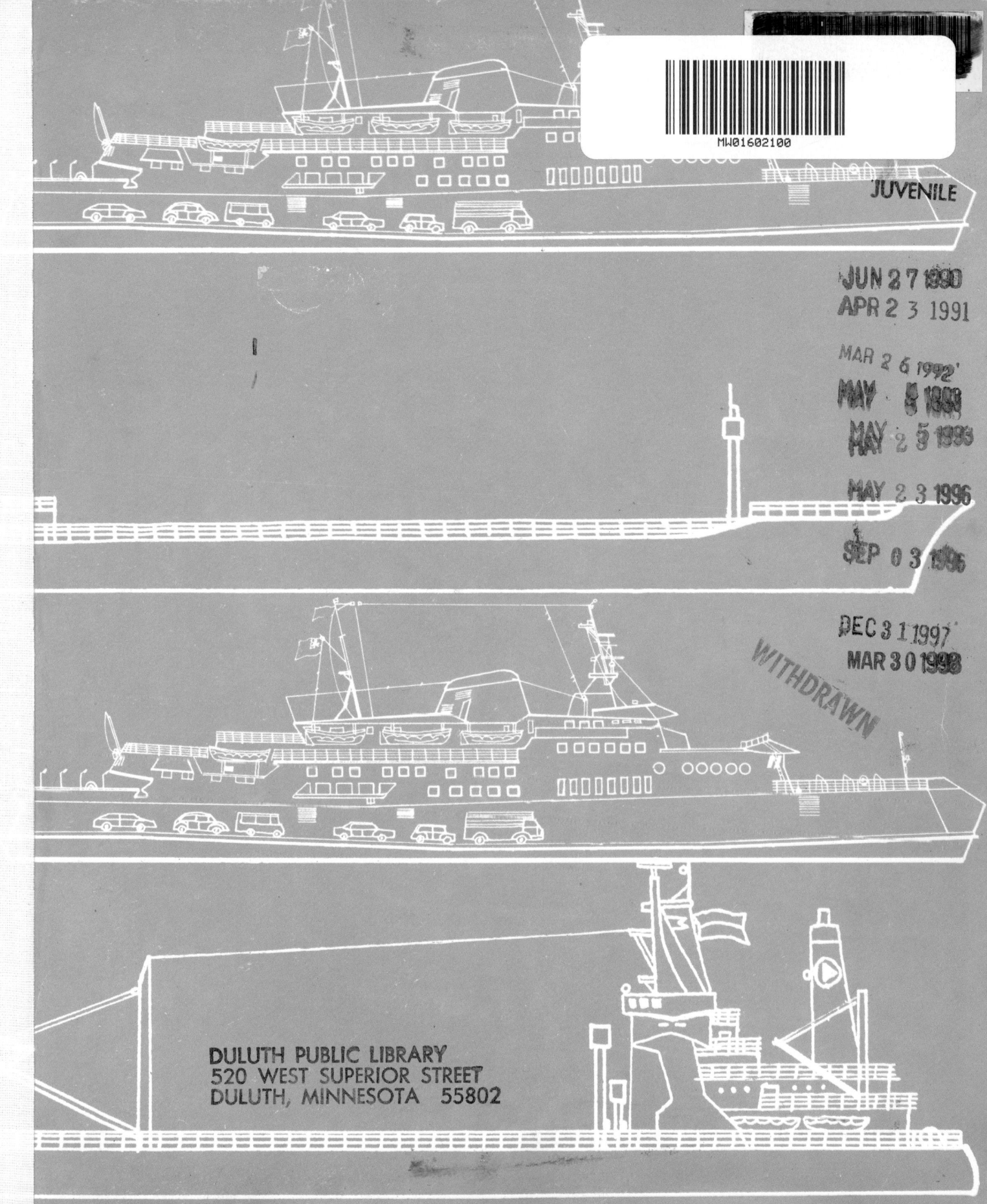

JUVENILE

A Read and Build Book

Ports
&
Harbours

Victoria Prego de Oliver

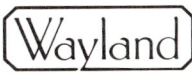

TEXT:
Victoria Prego de Oliver
Juan Ramón Azaola
TRANSLATION:
Lucilla Watson
MODELS:
María Cheridi
ILLUSTRATIONS:
Alberto Fernández, Ulises Wensell
PHOTOGRAPHS:
Lea Levi, Goyenechea, Salmer, Oronoz,
Europa Press, Flash Press, Peréz Triano,
Junta del Puerto de la Ría de Bilbao,
Port Autonome du Havre,
Port Autonome de Marseilles,
Novosti Picture Agency, Australian Embassy, Madrid
Kockums Dockyards, Mekanista Verkstads,
Gloria Lolivier (Centre International de
Realisations Iconographiques)
DESIGN:
Luis Agromayor, Paloma G. Amezúa
RESEARCH:
Carmen Aragonés
CO-ORDINATION:
Victoria Prego de Oliver
EDITED BY:
Miguel Azaola

ISBN 0 85340 632 4

Phototypeset by
Trident Graphics Limited
Printed in Spain by
PURESA — Badalona (Barcelona)
Dep. legal B-29.796-1978

Contents

About this book

This book has been written with the aim of explaining to you the workings of a port, one of those large ports with installations and warehouses stretching to the horizon and each day receiving hundreds of boats from all over the world. Many of us have had the opportunity of seeing one of these large ports; they have made us marvel, but their internal workings are beyond the reach of everyone not connected with the world of the sea and navigation.

Throughout these pages, you will be able to form an idea of what a port is and of the different kinds of boats and their uses; you will be able to identify all the buildings which are lined up in the port and form streets like a city within a city; you will come to understand the use and the workings of the enormous machines installed on quaysides. All this information is backed up by a large number of colour photographs and drawings which will help you to understand the text.

The aim of this book, however, is not con-fined to introducing you to the different parts making up a port. It should also help you to build some of the things illustrated in the photographs yourself. And it is because of this that in some of the chapters you will find suggestions on making models of some of the features that make up a port. You will also find a chapter on how to make a model of a large port, including the quays, boats, warehouses and harbour railway.

All these models can be made out of materials that are easy to obtain and to use such as wood, plastic and string. Making the models is also very simple. Of the things that you will build, some will work on the same principle – simplified, of course – as the one on which the real machines work. Other projects, like the model of the port, can be used as toys to which you can add things that you already possess. There will also be some things that you can use in the model, and in this way you will become an active participant in the daily life of the port.

S.O.S : Ship in distress!

The storm which for two days had been violently churning the sea is hardly noticeable in the inner harbour of the large port. Only the restless movement of the dark waters, the constant gusts of wind and the rain tirelessly beating down on the quays and sheds give a hint of the furious lashing of the seas against dykes and breakwaters further out. As night falls, the tempest makes the feeble lights in the port blink and sways the numerous boats that have come to berth there until the storm abates.

It is 9.25 p.m. when the alarm sounds. A radio message is received in the harbourmaster's office. It is a call for help from the cargo ship *Mauritius* sailing under the Liberian flag. As the result of serious damage to her rudder, she is drifting in mid-storm at 30km west-north-west. The message is immediately relayed to the salvage-tug station where there are crews on call round the clock.

In a few seconds, the engines of the most powerful tug are started up; while the alarm siren is still screaming, there is a desperate to-ing and fro-ing on the deck of the *Proctor* as the crew members hurry to their posts. The ropes tying the boat to the mooring posts on the quay are undone, the powerful lights are switched on and the steam siren is sounded, piercing the darkness of this unpleasant night. The *Proctor*'s captain gives the order for full power ahead and the boat begins to cut through the waters; this procedure is a familiar one, for the boat has travelled this path a thousand times. It decisively makes for the

harbour narrows, from there it enters the open sea.

The men on the tug know what is in store for them out there: waves 7 or 8 metres high churned up by a gale-force wind, and rain falling in sheets will beat down upon the bridge and cause the boat to rock terrifyingly in the darkness. But dealing with such a situation is part of their job. They fear the storm, but are determined to reach their objective. Moreover, it is not the first time that they and their boat have carried out this work under such conditions.

In fact, the *Proctor* is an excellent salvage tug with a brilliant record of service. It is equipped with a very powerful engine, the most modern systems of communication, lifeboats and towing mechanisms, and its manoeuverability is excellent. But perhaps the

Proctor's best piece of equipment is its crew, which is made up of the best and most experienced sailors.

The tug, now approaching the entrance to the port, is tossing more and more violently. The men, clad in their yellow oilskins and preparing the equipment in the cabin, are beginning to be sprayed by the first waves of the choppy sea. They will soon have to take cover or else face the storm resolutely . . .

Aboard the *Mauritius*, which is being led a sinister dance by the storm, the men are filled with an anxious hope. They know that their S.O.S. has been received and that a tug is coming to their aid. But only a few among them trust the already aged hull of the 4,000-tonne merchant vessel to stand up to the pounding of the waves until her rescuers arrive; neither is the crew sure that the sal-vage tug will be able to reach the *Mauritius* with the sea in such a state. Apart from this, no other boat seems to have received their message. There must be no one sailing in their vicinity. They are alone in this watery hell. For many members of the crew, this will be the longest night of their lives.

And as if that were not enough, a new and serious mishap has come to worsen the situation. A large part of the cargo of wood loaded on the bridge is swept overboard by a wave. The balance is upset and the *Mauritius* is list-ing dangerously to starboard. There is only one thing to do: the rest of the cargo must be jettisoned. To do this, the crew must go up onto the deck and slash the cables holding the cargo on the starboard side. The waves them-selves will then wash away the logs and restore the balance of the vessel.

9

Two brave volunteers, the boatswain and a sailor, go up onto the deck, each holding an axe and each firmly attached to the bridge by ropes. As far as the ship's position and the rocking of the waves allow, they deliver well-aimed blows to the logs piled up on the starboard side. The first freed logs soon fall into the sea. Slowly, the balance is restored. The waves continue to lighten the load. But now comes the real danger: the boat no longer being weighed down to starboard, the pitching starts anew and a dozen logs roll madly to and fro about the deck. The two men begin to step back towards the bridge, but a log knocks the boatswain over. Before any more logs follow suit, two men dash towards him and pick him up; he is unconscious.

For the moment the worst has been avoided. The crucial moment has passed and, while the ship's doctor is trying to revive the boatswain in the first-aid room, anxiety and uncertainty return to descend upon the men of the *Mauritius*.

It will be hours before a small crack of light appears on the horizon announcing the dawn. It is when the storm seems to have reached its peak that a distant light, intermittently obscured by the waves, can be made out. It is the tug! The captain gives orders for flares to be lit to signal their position. Then the two boats communicate by radio and confirm that they have seen one another.

The *Proctor* is already only 200 metres away from the heaving green-and-white mass

of the cargo vessel. At this distance the tug goes about and puts its engines into reverse. At less than 100 metres from the *Mauritius*, it stops. It would be dangerous to come closer with the sea in this state; the ship could at any moment lurch forward and crush the tug. The salvage crew will now try to throw a line to the *Mauritius* by means of a rocket. This is not an easy operation: on the lower deck of the tug, a man whom the waves lash relentlessly fires a rocket with a fine nylon rope attached. But the blustering wind blows it off course and it ends up in the sea. A second attempt produces the same result. So does a third. The captain of the *Proctor* gives orders

to approach the ship by a few more metres. The fourth attempt is successful. But with this success comes a moment of anxiety, chilling the hearts of both the crews: a gigantic wave visibly moves the cargo vessel forwards. The crew of the tug see the massive ship towering above them. Just as collision seems unavoidable they are themselves carried forward by the same wave. Five metres more and the crash would have been disastrous!

From the *Mauritius*, the fine rope is being hauled in, followed by progressively thicker rope until the long sturdy steel towing cable is reached. It is now that a very powerful winch must be used to take the great weight of the cable which the *Proctor*, by slowly moving forward, feeds out to a length of many metres. When the cables have been submerged to a

11

sufficient depth to deaden the jerks between the two vessels, the tug moves forward about 1,000 metres. It must be nearly five o'clock in the morning before the boats can begin the journey back to port. With the dawn, the rough sea looks more spectacular but becomes less terrifying. It is still raining . . .

"Hello! Harbour-master's office? We are coming into port with the *Mauritius* on tow. Are you receiving me? Over."

"We hear you, *Proctor*. Good work! Anything to report? Over."

"The others have one casualty, but we are all right. We've done it again this time."

"Should we pick up the casualty by coast-guard helicopter? Over."

"No; it doesn't look too serious – just a heavy blow and a broken arm. What's the weather forecast? Over."

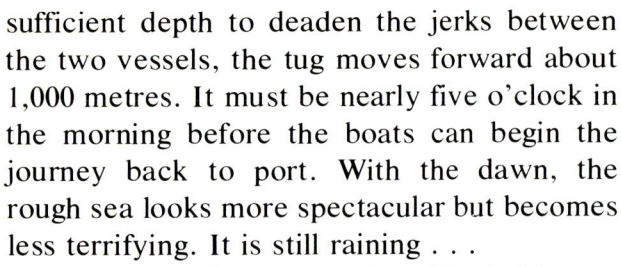

"Well, it seems that we will be blown about for a good while yet. Over."

"Understood. I hope to be there in six hours. Over and out."

At 10.45 the boats make their way through the entrance to the harbour, between whose arms the fury of the storm dies down. The *Proctor* emits two long siren calls and for a moment all attention in the harbour is turned towards the boats.

Aboard the two vessels, anxiety has given way to relief among the exhausted crew members. They look about them in silence: boats, quays, wharves, cranes, warehouses, roads, moorings, bollards, berths, workshops. Not one of them breathes a word, but they are probably all thinking the same thing: "We have come home . . . to the home of all boats . . . to the home of all of us."

13

How to make a model of a natural harbour

MATERIALS

A sheet of plywood about 90×100cm

Some corrugated cardboard or cork

A sheet of blue, transparent plastic

Paper and pieces of cloth

Tissue paper and sawdust

Plastic wood

Glue

Paint and green dye

TOOLS

A pair of scissors

A paintbrush

A sieve

You will use the model of a natural bay, which is the first piece of work to be done, as a base for the other things that you will make to turn it into a man-made harbour. In this first stage, the correct preparation of the sheet of wood on which you are going to work is very important.

1. The first and most important thing to do is to glue several strips of cork or corrugated cardboard to one side of the sheet of plywood, as shown in the drawing.

You should apply glue to both sides to be stuck and take care that they stay firmly glued together.

Place the plywood on a flat surface, pile some heavy books on top of it and wait for the glue to dry.

This step is important because it will stop the plywood warping from contact with wet glue and with the other substances which you will use later on.

2. In blue ink or soft pencil, draw the outline of the sea coast and the bay on the other side of the plywood. Draw in the natural irregularities as you like, since the bay does not have to be perfectly uniform.

You will find it easier to place the features on the model if you rule a grid on the plywood before you start to draw. On the outline you can already mark the places chosen for the different things that will make up the finished port:

O: centre of bay; A and B: harbour narrows; C: container area; D: fishing harbour and marina; E and F: ferry quays; G: main quay; H: bridge and barge quay.

Place the sheet of transparent blue plastic for the water over this drawing and trace the outline onto it.

Then cut it out and leave it to one side for the moment.

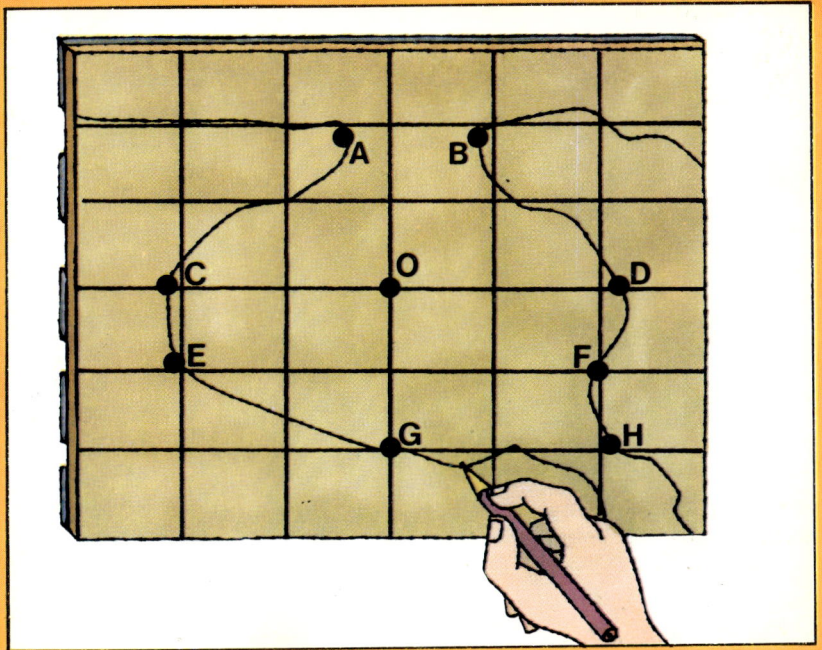

3. In the places intended for the hills enclosing the bay, fix some balls of paper which have been lightly coated with glue.

Cover them with pieces of cloth which have been well soaked in carpenters' or white glue and shape them to look like hills, giving the slopes the irregularities you like (for example, one or two caves on the sea side, a level area to accommodate a house or beacon, etc.).

Take care that the pieces of cloth do not overlap the outline of the sea that you have drawn. It is even better if they fall short.

15

4. While the pieces of cloth are drying, take the piece of transparent blue plastic that you cut out earlier and glue it over the area reserved for the sea.

If some space between the foot of the mountains and the waterline remains uncovered, fill it in with plastic wood. You can also glue some sand on your model and some pebbles to look like rocks.

5. Take some pieces of corrugated cardboard, which you can find in packing material or buy at a stationer's, and cover the whole area of dry land not taken up by the mountains. You can also use thin sheets of cork.

Glue these pieces carefully and place a weight on them to prevent warping and to stop the cardboard coming unstuck.

The area of dry land will thus be slightly higher than the level of the sea. On this area, we are going to build the installations and roads common to every modern port.

16

6.   Take a little plastic wood, obtainable at any do-it-yourself shop, and wet it with a few drops of water.
   While it is still moist, spread it all round the cut edge of the cardboard or cork, following the outline of the sea.
   If you like, you can model a few irregularities, making the paste overlap slightly on the blue plastic.

7.   Before going any further, take some yellow or brown paint and colour the pieces of cloth making the hills. The coat of paint must be thick enough for the cloth to be completely soaked.
   So that the hills should not look too uniform, you could touch them up with a few strokes of a darker colour, but always after the last coat has dried.

17

8. Buy some imitation grass in a modelling shop, cut it to shape and carefully glue it over the whole area of cardboard or cork.

If you are unable to find this kind of imitation grass, you can give a realistic effect with sawdust dyed green.

To dye the sawdust, put it in a sieve and dip it into a container filled with green paint or clothes dye. Gently shake the sieve, lift it out, and let it drip. Spread the sawdust out to dry on a piece of plastic or newspaper.

After it has been dyed, glue it all over the area of cardboard and scatter a little over the mountains.

9. Already the model is nearly finished.

If you want the edges to look smooth and tidy, spread some plastic wood all round the model, carefully filling in the holes of the corrugated cardboard that you glued to the sheet of plywood.

You can buy plastic wood at do-it-yourself shops. Spread it round the edges of the model while it is still wet, then leave it to dry.

10. The trees of the model are made up of little sticks painted brown with a piece of sponge fixed to one end.

   If you prefer, you can use pieces of green cellophane paper or moss instead of sponge.

   You can also paint the pieces of sponge dark red or yellow, the colour of leaves in autumn.

   Lastly, place the trees where you like on the model and nail them into the ground. If you like, you can also scatter some pebbles about to look like rocks and boulders wherever you think they will be suitable.

This is the finished model of the natural bay. Notice how the hills have been arranged. The trees have already been placed on the model, but you can put yours wherever you like.

From port to superport

A modern port is a vast transit complex for all kinds of goods, a gigantic crossroads where all the flags of the world are flown and all languages heard . . .

Open to the high seas, colourful and cosmopolitan centres where ships from all over the world come in to berth, ports have since earliest times symbolised a country's commercial wealth.

The natural harbour. *Every large modern port was in its beginnings many, many years ago nothing more than a peaceful, sheltered bay of blue water; and the town surrounding every great port began as a fishing village whose inhabitants ventured no further than a few kilometres out to sea for the sole purpose of catching enough fish to feed the community. Later, people set out across the sea in search of other populations, with whom they exchanged their goods. This trade made these places prosperous towns and villages.*

A primitive way of loading. *Right: Egyptian slaves carrying cargo to two merchant ships.*

For a long time, cargo was loaded and unloaded near the shore. Slaves were used to do this work, and, at times with the water up to their necks, they would carry huge jars of wine and oil, sacks of grain and bundles of textiles.

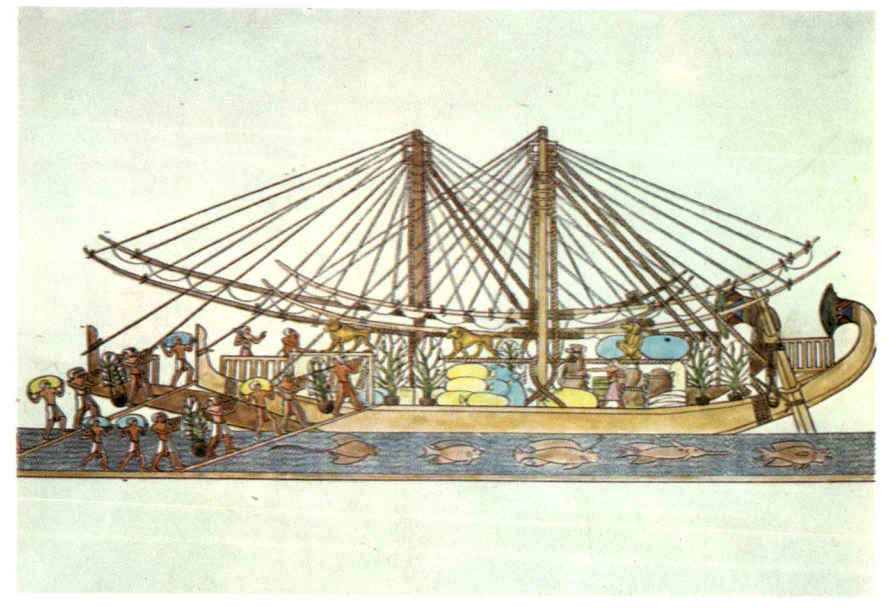

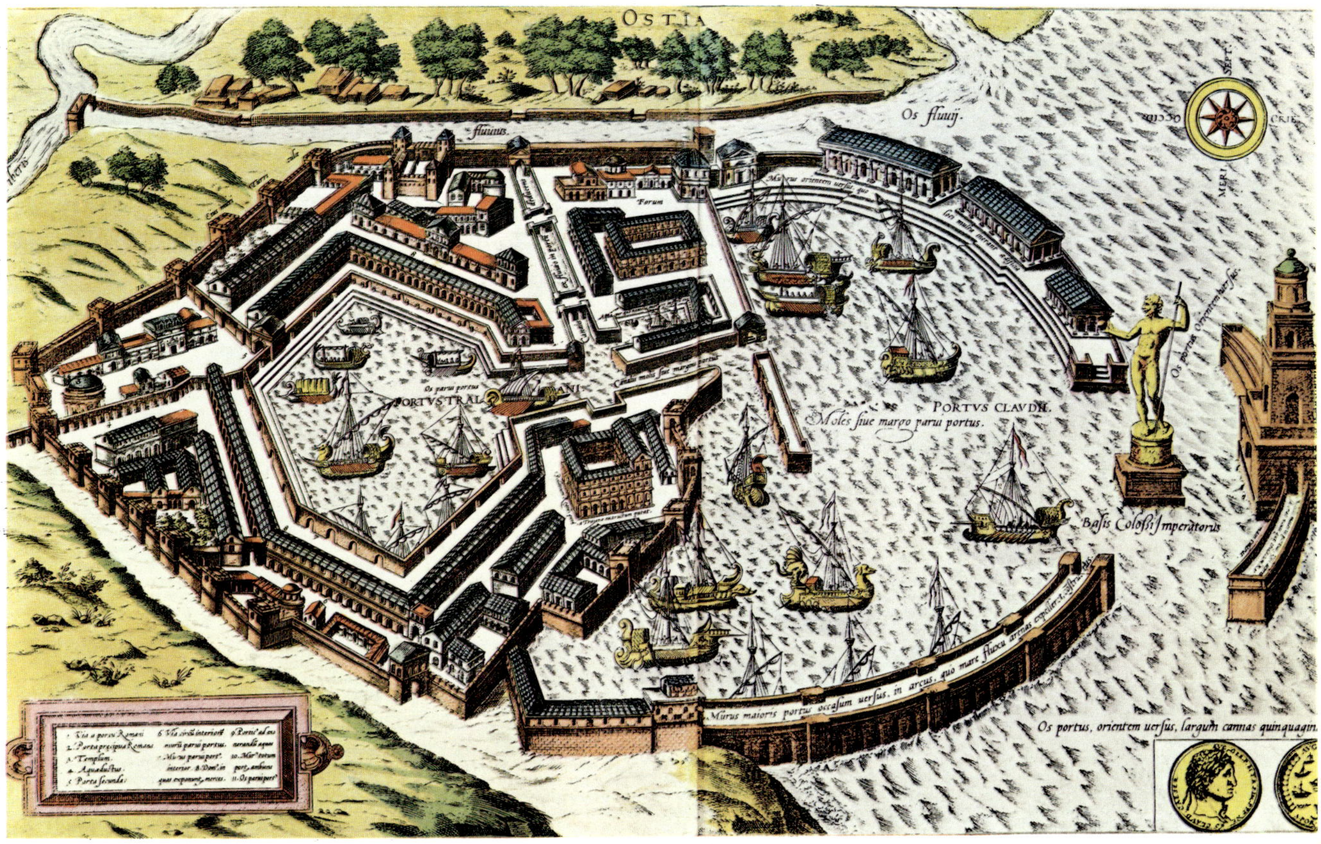

Fortified ports. *Many ports were fortified to protect the great riches massed on their quays against raids by pirates. Above, the Roman port of Ostia, situated near the imperial capital.*

Many other ports, such as Rhodes, Nice, Genoa and La Rochelle, were built in this way at various periods in history.

Quays and piers. *When piracy died out and, with it, the threat that it posed to the goods stored in ports, transport by sea reached an unprecedented peak.*

Fortifications were no longer needed and ports became the most important centres for trade between countries.

Longer quays were built to accommodate all the goods which arrived. But it was in the 19th century that the building of large piers began on a large scale and with the help of advanced construction techniques.

21

Roman merchant vessel (2nd century A.D.*)*

Egyptians, Phoenicians, Greeks, Vikings . . . all were excellent sailors who made important contributions to the techniques of navigation.

The Greeks were the first to build a port on the open sea: the port of Alexandria which in the 3rd century B.C. already possessed jetties eight kilometres long.

As to the Phoenicians, they came to be the only sea power in the Mediterranean until the 8th century B.C. The Vikings were also expert sailors, who in the course of their travels by sea discovered Iceland and Greenland and reached Sicily.

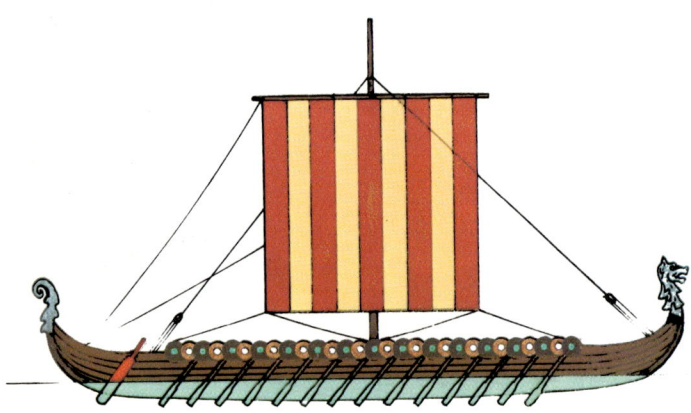

Viking longship (9th century)

Spanish galleon, 16th century

The contrast between industrial progress and the centuries-old methods of navigation is symbolised in the gigantic "Great Eastern" (1858), which is both steamboat and sailing ship.

Sea trade. *The method of powering ships by steam drastically cut the length of journeys by sea. This was a major advantage in the transport of perishable goods. Railways appeared round about the same time, and the combination of these two means of transport led to an even greater increase in sea trade. Because of this, ports became important centres of cultural exchange.*

Right, steamboats lined up in the port of New Orleans and awaiting the cargo which they will carry to the other side of the Atlantic.

A modern trading port. *A modern port differs greatly in appearance from the ports of an earlier age. The funnels of steamboats and the heaping of goods on the quays in the open air have disappeared. They have been replaced by gigantic cranes and enormous buildings. Below, ships docked in the port of Southampton.*

How to make a man-made harbour

MATERIALS
Balsa wood
Felt
A sheet of cardboard
Some small sticks
Rug-making canvas
Gloss paints
Glue
Small, round-headed nails

TOOLS
A penknife
Some sandpaper
A paintbrush
Scissors

Onto the natural bay you have already made, you are now going to fit all the features characteristic of a large modern port: quays, railways, buildings and roads. You do not have to make the model exactly the same as the one shown in this book. You can place each piece where you like.

1. Make a plan of the natural bay and draw in the outlines of all the features which make up a man-made harbour: the container wharves (A), the ferry quay (E), the commercial and petrol wharf (C), the pier (D), the fishing quays (B), the railway lines (1, 2, 3), the road (4) and its junction (5) and the lorry park (6). When you draw in the railway lines, remember that they must lead to each quay. Also see that the road runs behind the quays, passing close to the edge of the model.

This plan is only to give you a rough idea of how to lay out the port. You can make any changes you think necessary.

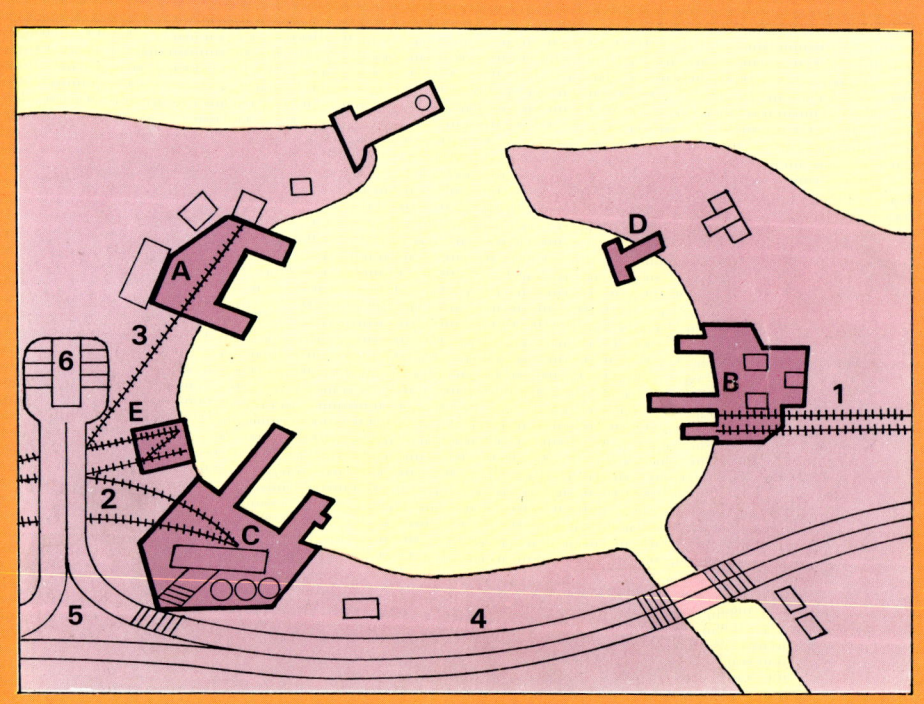

2.   Now begin to build the container wharf. Take a piece of strong material or some felt and draw the outline of the wharf onto it, following the measurements given in the drawing.

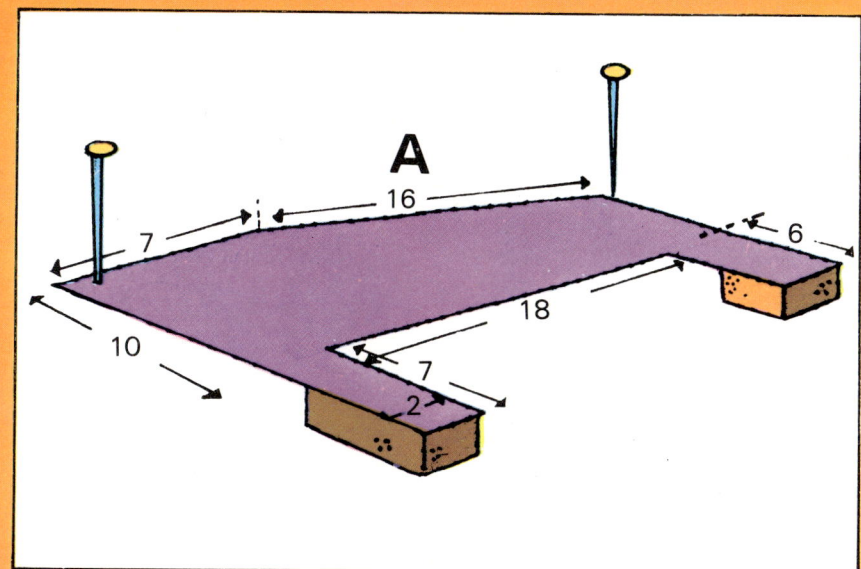

Cut out the material and glue it to a piece of cardboard to reinforce the wharf.

Where the arms of the wharf stretch out to the sea, glue two pieces of wood underneath the material. In this way, the dock will remain on the same level when you place it on the model.

3.   The procedure for building the fishing quay is the same as the one explained above, except that the shape is different.

Roughly following the measurements given in the drawing, cut out a piece of felt the same colour as the one you used for the container wharf, and glue it to a piece of cardboard.

This time, there are three pieces of wood to glue underneath the felt.

This quay, like all the others and like the road as well, is fixed to the model with round-headed nails which, neatly pushed in, will double-up as beacons. The heads can be painted red or yellow, or, if you prefer, you can use nails with heads of different colours.

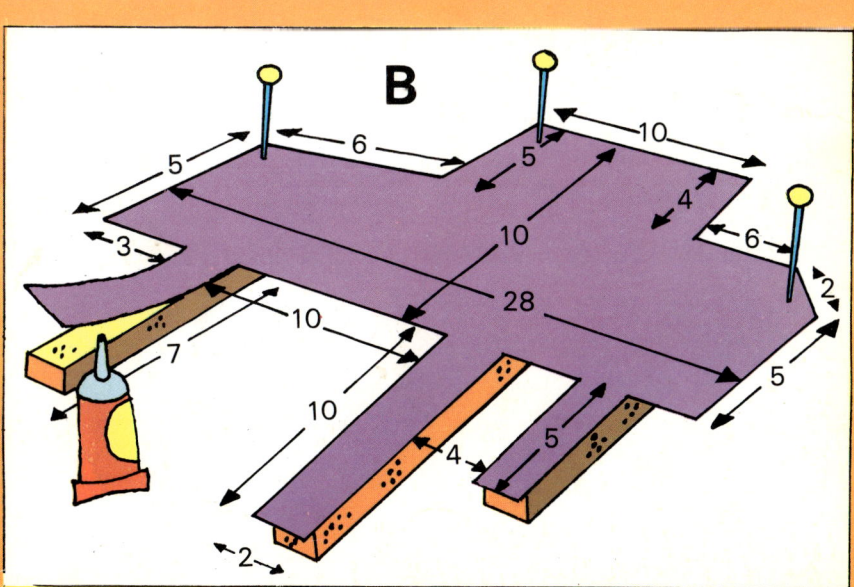

25

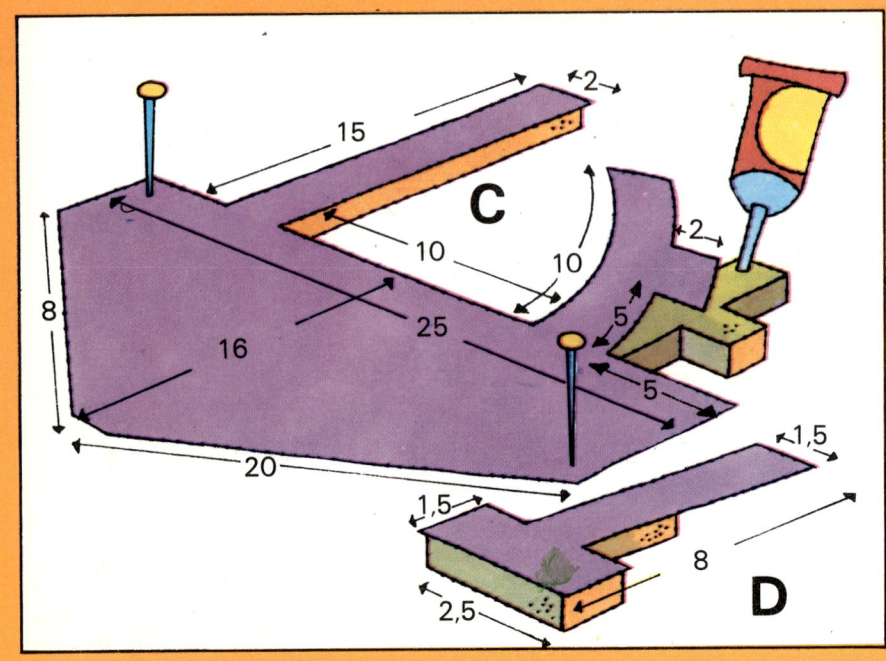

4. Now build the quay where cargo vessels and petrol tankers will come to berth, and the jetty for small boats.

Use the same method as for the other quays, but do not forget that the pieces of wood to be glued underneath the felt are for keeping the whole quay on the same level.

This means that they should fit the projections perfectly without sticking out at the sides.

5. The ferry dock is the simplest to make: it consists of a rectangle of felt 6×12cm, reinforced with a piece of cardboard cut to the same size, and a piece of wood glued at one end of the underside.

This quay should be placed at the same level as the ferry's loading zone so that the railway trucks can run straight to the hold of the vessel.

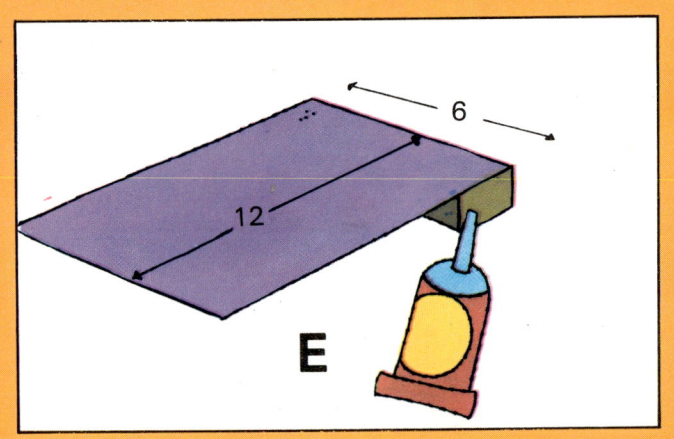

6. To fix the quays onto the model, follow these instructions: coat the underside of the pieces of wood with strong glue and place them on the surface of the sea. As we have already seen, the part of the quay resting on land is to be secured with round-headed nails.

Glue some narrow strips of coloured cloth onto the wide part of the quays to mark the spots where the cranes are to go later on.

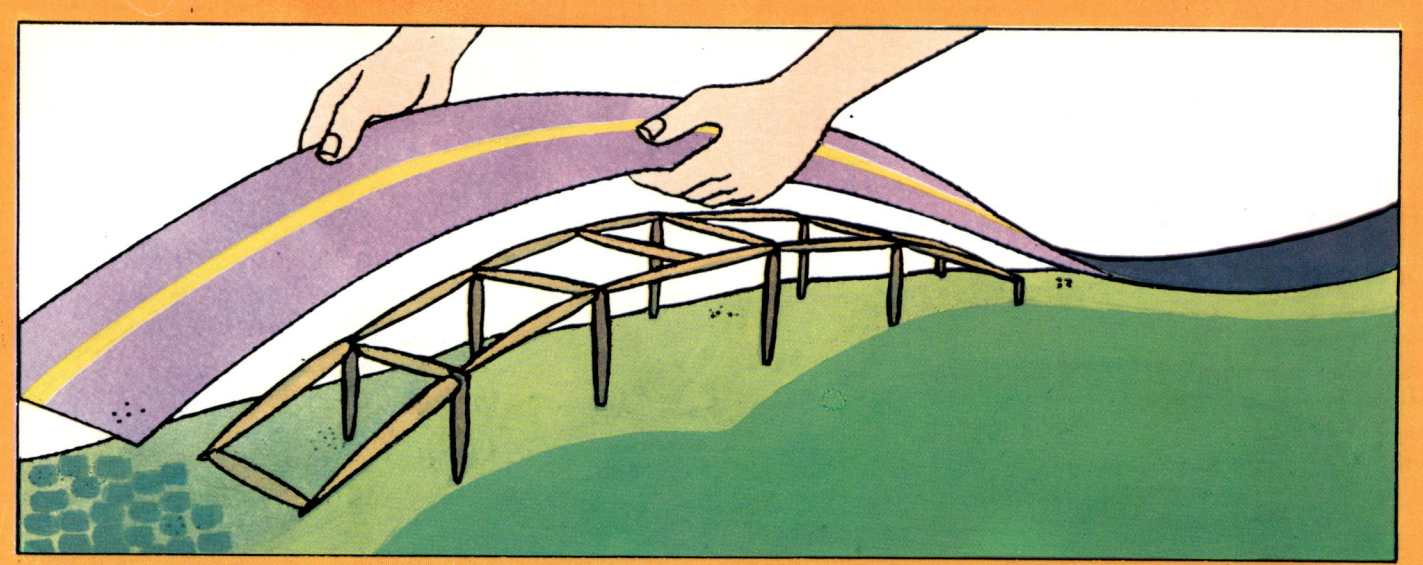

7.   Now now it is time to build a raised support so that the railway lines can pass underneath the road which you will soon be making.

   Take several round-headed sticks, clip the ends and glue them to one another, as shown in the drawing. Begin by gluing all the sticks making up one side, giving it a rounded shape. Then glue the crosswise sticks. Make the other side separately and fix it to the crosswise sticks. Lastly, attach the supporting sticks.

   The structure supporting the raised road is now finished.

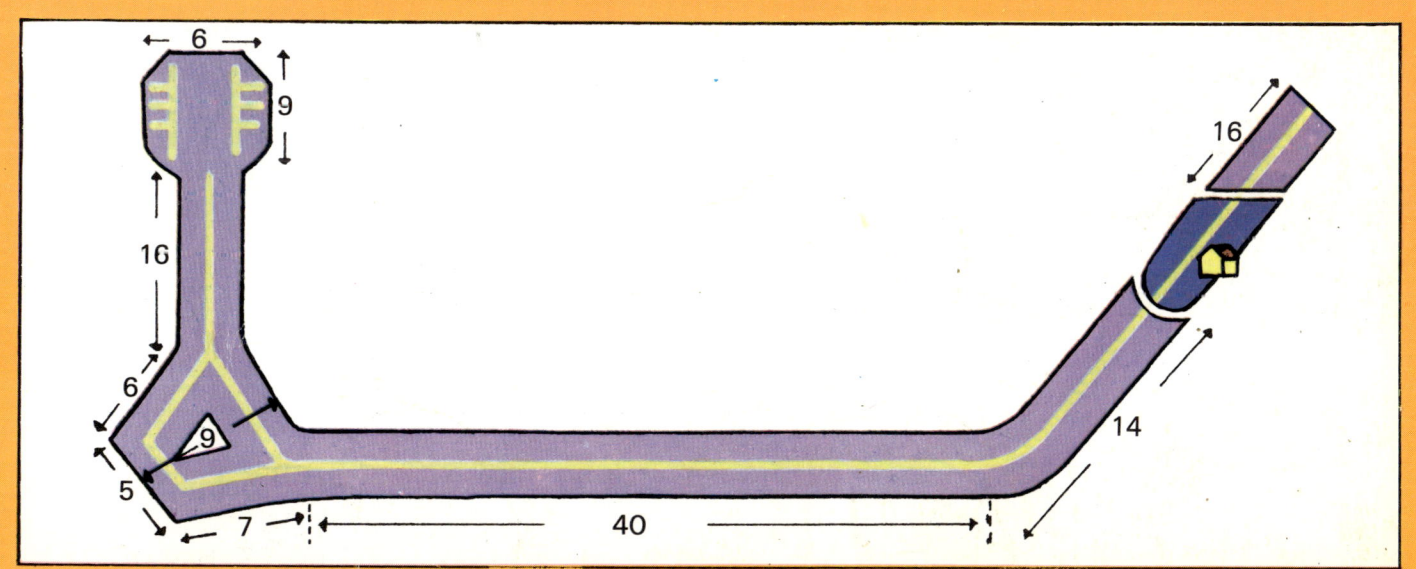

8.   To make the road, cut out a strip of felt 2.5cm wide to run round the model behind the quays. If you do not have a large enough piece, cut out several and glue them end to end.

   Before drawing the outline onto the felt, look carefully at the plan of the port: the road widens at one end to accommodate the lorry park and is interrupted at the other as it comes to the river.

   When you have cut it out, paint a yellow line down the middle, pin it to the model with round-headed nails and lay it over the raised support which you made in paragraph 7 above.

9. This is the swing bridge across the river.

Take a penknife and cut out a piece of balsa wood 10cm long, 2.5cm wide and 7mm high. Rub one end with sandpaper until it is rounded and cut the other end at an angle. Glue a strip of felt to the upper side and paint a yellow line down the centre.

Attach a strip of wood to each side of the bridge.

About 1.5cm from the rounded end, pierce a hole right through the wood. Push a long nail through the hole and down to a depth of a few millimetres into the ground beneath. This will be the axis on which the bridge will turn. Lastly, place the watchman's hut, carved from a block of balsa wood, on one side.

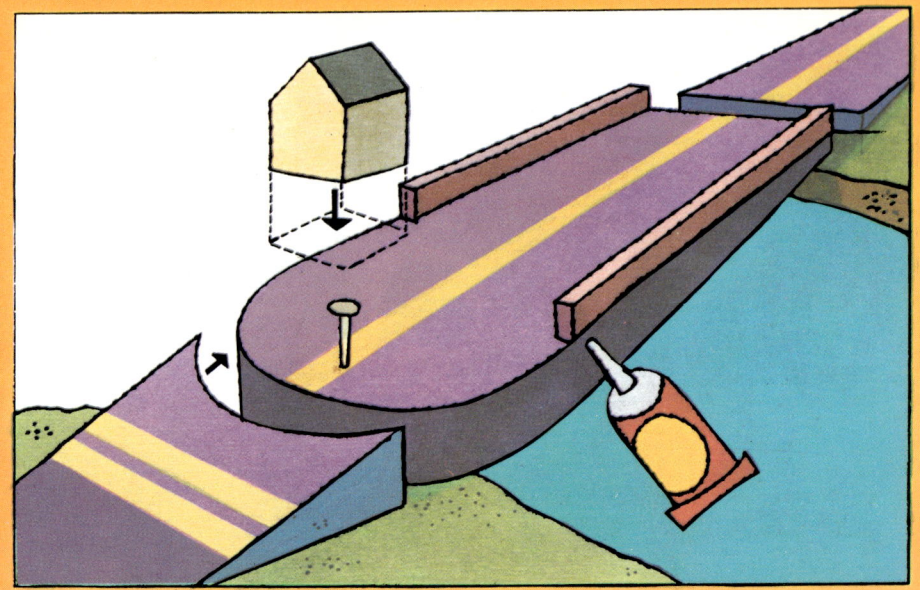

10. Take the end of the road leading to the swing bridge and raise it on a wedge of wood, which should be concave at the front, as shown in the drawing. To give the wedge its concave shape, first draw the arc of a circle onto it. With a penknife, cut the wood along the line you have drawn. Cut the end of the felt road to the concave shape of the wedge, then glue it down.

This slope has been built to make the road level with the swivel bridge so that cars can drive across without difficulty.

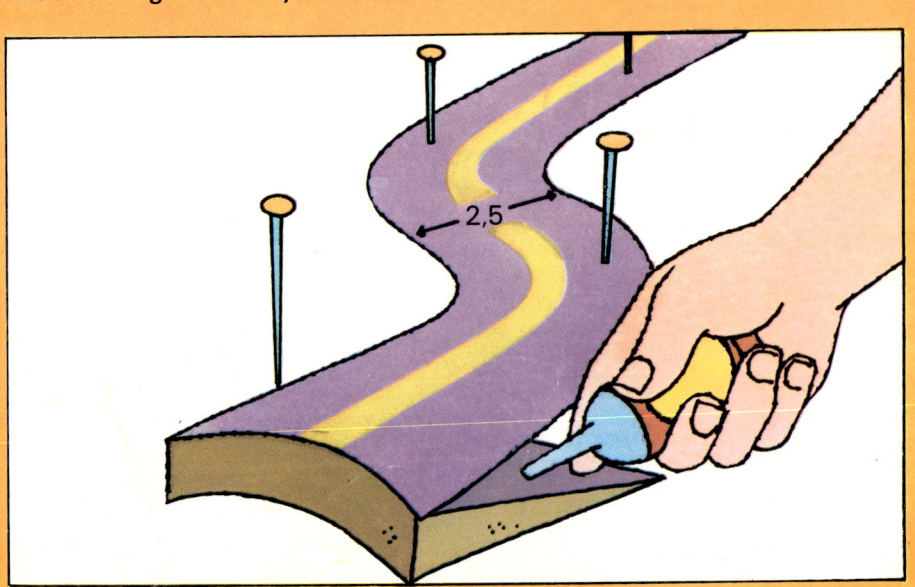

11. The railway lines are easy to make.

Buy a piece of canvas of the kind used for rug making. Cut it into narrow strips, as shown in the illustration, in such a way that they look like rails.

To see what shape they should be cut to in order to reach the quays, study the plan which appears at the beginning of this chapter. Then paint the railways brown and place them in position as shown in the plan or wherever you think best.

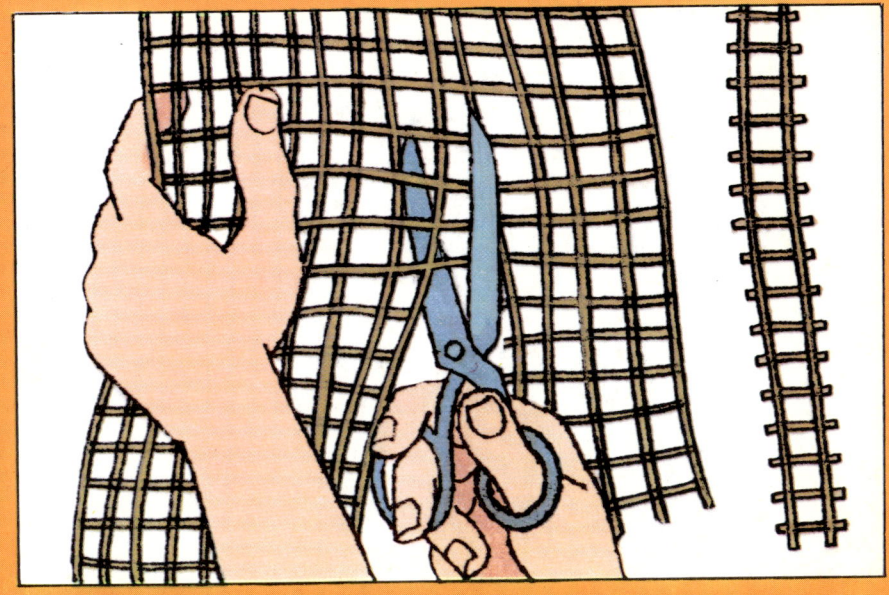

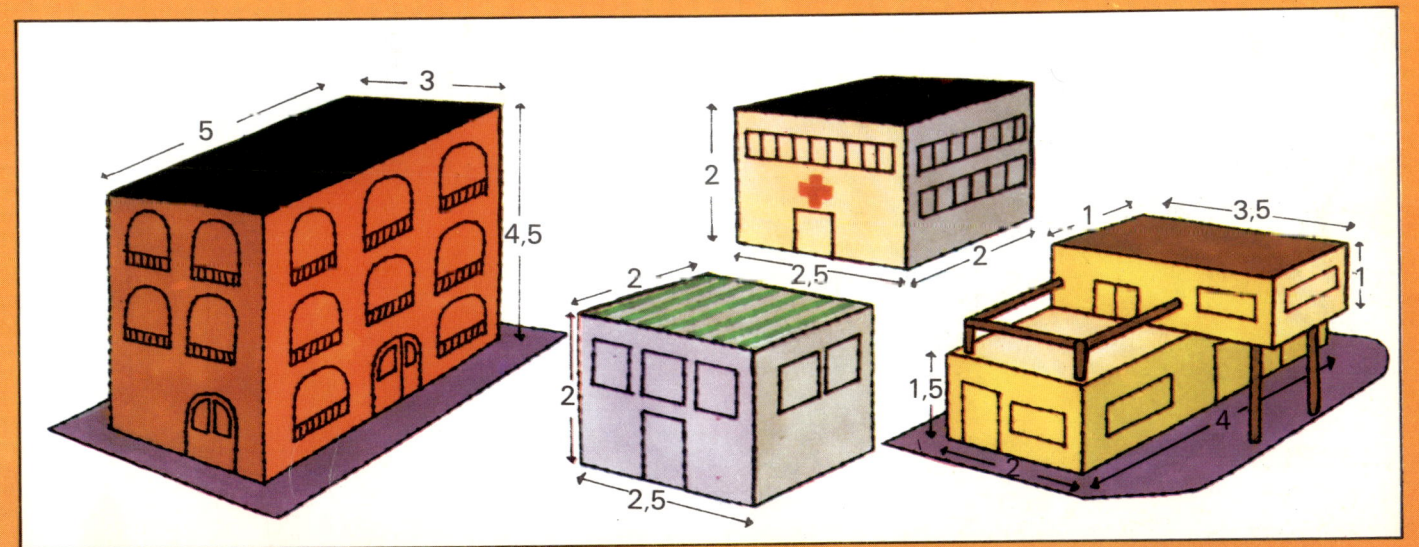

12. This illustration shows the harbour-master's office, the first-aid building, a cottage for the fishing village, and the sailing club. Make them out of balsa wood, following the measurements given. Remember that you will need to make several fishermen's cottages to complete the village.

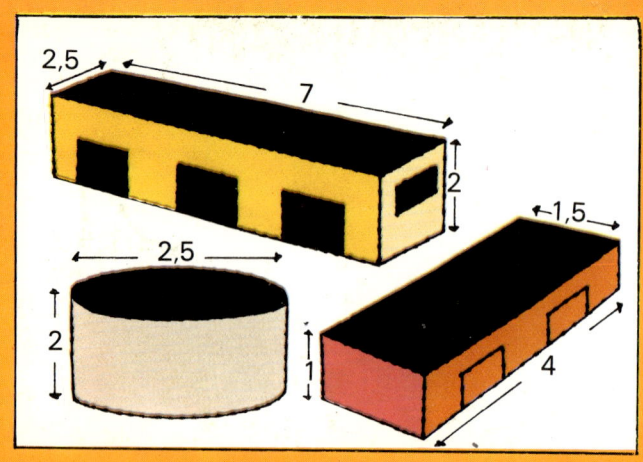

13.   These are the goods depots and fuel tank. They are also made out of balsa wood and may be painted with any kind of paint.

Remember that these are only examples and that you should make several of each one.

14.   Make a fleet of lorries as well, built to your own design. As suggestions, we have shown four models which you can copy and reproduce several times if they appeal to you. If you use cork or soft wood such as balsa, you will be able to make the lorries out of a single block.

15.   The locomotive for the goods train is made out of several pieces of wood glued together. The wheels are little round pieces of felt glued onto pieces of cardboard of the same size. These are then glued to the sides of the locomotive.

For the goods trucks, make the base shown in the drawing and add blocks of wood 3×2cm.

16.   The locomotive for the tank wagons can also be made out of a single piece painted in two different colours. The wheels are pieces of felt the same as for the first train.

To build the tank wagons, make a few bases and glue a painted cigarette filter or a section of a pencil or a dowel onto each one.

This is a general view of the port with all its features in position. Each important part has been included in the model: the fishing harbour, commercial wharves, marina, etc. The size of the quays depends on the importance of their function in a typical port. This is why the commercial wharves are larger and the fishing harbour smaller. Notice too the lay-out of the railway lines and the way they run beneath the road, which is raised on a support. On one side of the port, the ferry acts as a link between the two opposite sides of the bay where the railway lines stop. The photograph on the right shows in detail the working of the swing bridge linking the two strips of road separated by the river. When a vessel wants to enter the bay from the river, or vice versa, the bridge swings round, briefly interrupting the flow of traffic on the road.

31

Navigation in the harbour

Because the size of modern ships is increasing every day, the difficulty of navigating inside harbours is also becoming greater. Often, the entrance channels are not deep enough; the quays are no longer able to receive so many ships, so that vessels must await their turn; the space given them to berth in is usually reduced to a minimum.

To solve all these problems and the many others that navigation inside a harbour presents today, teams of men and modern signalling systems work together. Both make it easier for ships to enter and berth.

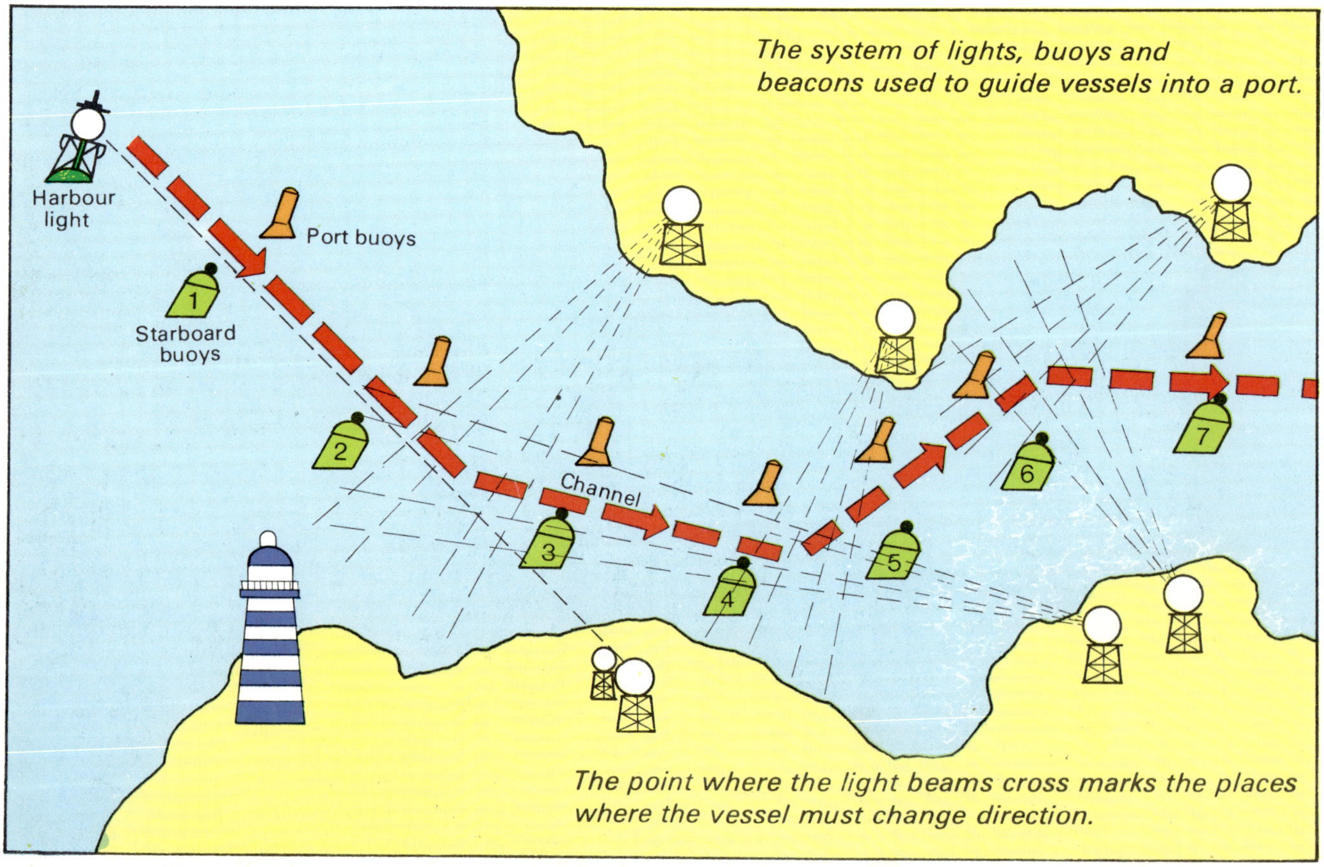

The system of lights, buoys and beacons used to guide vessels into a port.

Harbour light

Port buoys

Starboard buoys

1

2

3

4

5

6

7

Channel

The point where the light beams cross marks the places where the vessel must change direction.

The entrance to the harbour. *So that a ship may reach the quay allotted to her without difficulty, her captain must rely on the assistance of lights, buoys, beacons, radar, tugs and, above all, on the invaluable experience of the harbour pilot.*

Below, on the opposite page, the beams of light which cross one another show the changes in direction the ship must make in order to follow the entrance channel. This complicated system of signalling is absolutely essential in river ports or closed bays like the Bay of San Francisco (right).

The pilot. *All ports, and especially those with a difficult approach, have a team of pilots with a thorough knowledge of the harbour in which they work. Every ship's captain must rely upon the help of the pilot when sailing into an unfamiliar harbour.*

When a vessel is about to enter a harbour, it requests the services of the pilot. The pilot then makes his way towards the ship aboard a launch marked with the letter P, indicating that it is the pilot's launch. When the launch has drawn up alongside the ship, the pilot climbs up a ladder to reach the bridge, where he takes over from the captain to steer the ship through the hazardous channel into port.

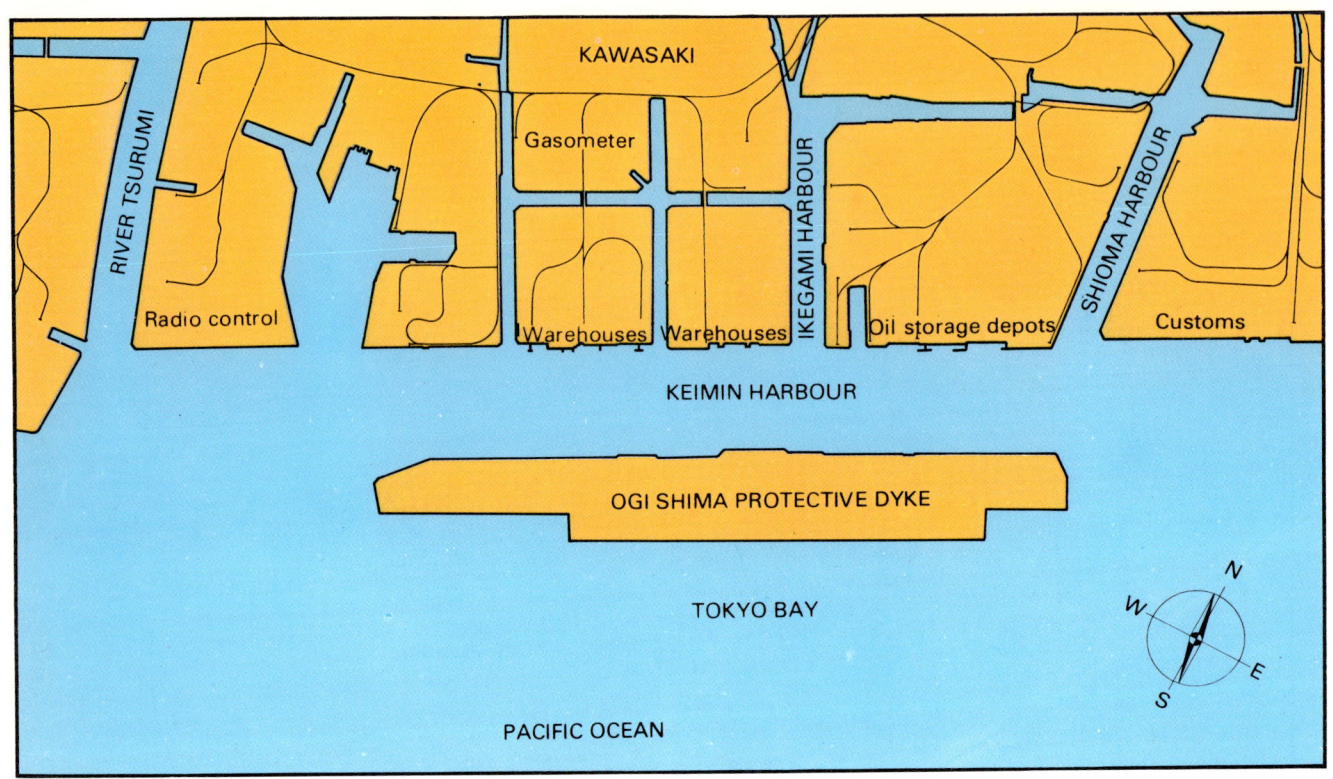

KAWASAKI

Gasometer

RIVER TSURUMI

IKEGAMI HARBOUR

SHIOMA HARBOUR

Radio control

Warehouses Warehouses

Oil storage depots

Customs

KEIMIN HARBOUR

OGI SHIMA PROTECTIVE DYKE

TOKYO BAY

N
W E
S

PACIFIC OCEAN

The tugs. *These are essential equipment in every harbour. Without their help large ships would never manage to steer themselves through the labyrinth of docks and canals of a port such as Yokohama (above). The tug takes over from the pilot to lead the ship in to berth. With its engines switched off, the ship lets itself be towed by means of a cable attached to a steel hook (below). The small craft then gently pushes the ship until it is in the right place (left).*

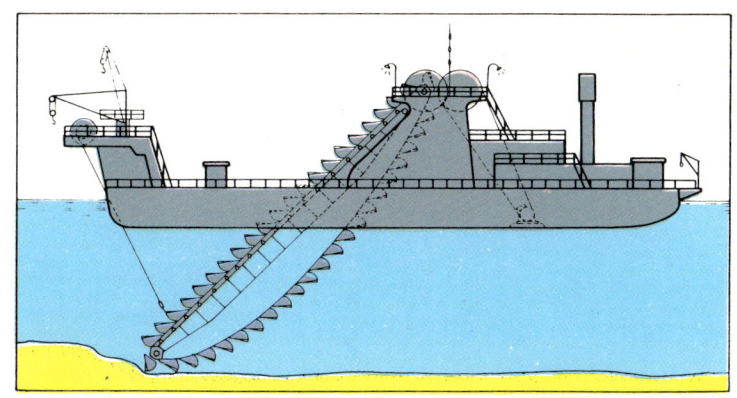

The increase in the draught of ships prevents many of them from entering certain harbours that are not deep enough. It also happens that the entrance channels become silted up with sand, weeds or rocks carried in by the water. To remedy the situation, the sea-bed must be dredged, or cleaned, with special machines. This is how a port is kept deep enough for most ships.

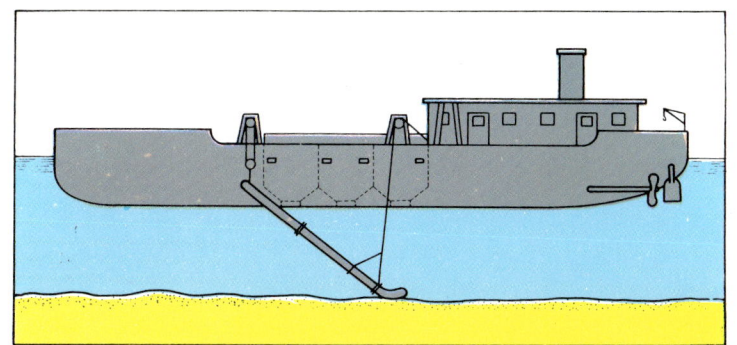

The dredgers. *These machines, which are specially designed to clean sea-beds, were invented by the Dutch, who for centuries have had to dredge their navigation channels constantly. The two illustrations on the left show a scoop-chain dredger designed to clear rocky bottoms (above), and a suction dredger used for sucking up mud and sand.*

Mooring. *Large ships need large amounts of space in which to manoeuvre. To avoid knocking against the walls of the quays, they first throw their hawsers to the harbour craft (below), which then carries them to posts, where they are secured by mooring teams. The photograph on the right shows a moored ship.*

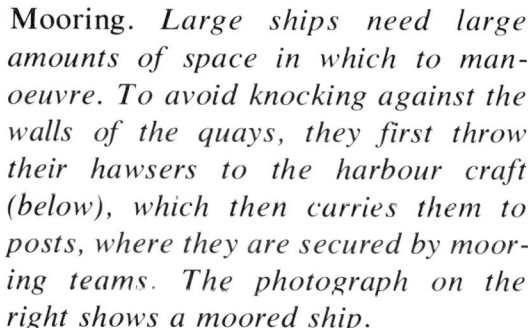

How to make some boats for the model

MATERIALS
  Balsa wood or cork
  Gloss paint of different colours
  Water-resistant glue
  Toothpicks
  Fine white cloth 10×5cm
  Sandpaper

TOOLS
  A penknife
  A pair of scissors
  A file
  A paintbrush

These little boats will bring the man-made harbour to life; without them it would seem dull and lifeless. You can make them out of balsa wood or cork and if you like you can make other boats different from the ones suggested here.

1. TRANSATLANTIC LINER. This vessel, like all the others in this chapter, can be made out of balsa wood or cork. Cut out the shape with a penknife and smooth it with sandpaper.

The funnels of this ship are pieces of wood attached with waterproof glue.

When you have made the liner, draw in the windows and portholes with a black marker and coat the hull in gloss paint.

2. CONTAINER VESSEL. The deck of container vessels is built at a lower level than in other ships and the bridge is placed nearer the poop so as to leave as much space as possible for the cargo which it will carry.

3.   OIL TANKER. A characteristic feature of tankers is their enormous length. They are by far the largest ships of all. Make yours out of a piece of cork or balsa wood about 15cm long and 2cm wide. Glue the pieces making up the bridge and the funnel, then paint them grey or black.

4.   CARGO SHIP. The cranes lined up on the deck of this ship distinguish it from the other types of vessel.

With a few matchsticks carefully arranged and glued on the deck, you can make some very lifelike cranes.

5.   TRAWLER. The fishing vessel is very easy to make. When you have shaped the hull, all you have to do is glue a piece of wood onto it; a little stick glued into place makes the funnel.

The masts are two toothpicks glued at each end of the ship; the sails are three triangles of cloth attached to the masts with a little glue.

6.   SAILING BOATS. These vessels are much smaller than the others illustrated here: they are no more than 3cm long. The masts and sails are also made out of toothpicks and triangles of cloth attached with glue.

7. FERRY. Take a piece of wood or cork 6cm long, 3cm wide and 1.5cm thick. Round it at the edges with sandpaper until it has the shape of the boat in the drawing.

Glue the two strips of wood for the railings each side of the boat. Place in position the pieces of wood making the cabin. To finish, cut out a piece of canvas of the kind used for making rugs and glue it onto the deck of the boat: these are the rails for the railway wagons.

8. BARGES. The barge is a type of vessel used for carrying cargo to the quays from boats that are unable to berth there. These vessels are relatively small; make them about 4 or 5cm long. The deck is designed to carry cargo. You can make the cargo out of a piece of wood painted in any colour and glued onto the barge. The cabin is also made out of a piece of wood or cork glued onto the prow.

9. FISHING BOATS AND BUOYS. These are the boats which are seen on many beaches of the world; they are used for fishing at a short distance from the shore. Make four or five of them, each 3cm long.

The buoys for the model are red rivets obtainable at a shoemaker's.

10. SEAPLANE. You will find it easier to make the fuselage of the seaplane out of cork first and then the wings out of a thin strip of wood. Make the wings rounded at the tip, then glue them either side of the aircraft.

Follow the same procedure for attaching the tailplane and the skids for alighting on water.

11.   PILOT'S LAUNCH, AMBULANCE CRAFT, AND TUG. The pilot's launch is narrow and tapering. Make it out of a single piece of wood and glue a short mast on top of the cabin; you can make the mast out of a matchstick.

Tugs are very short and wide. Their principal characteristic is that they are much higher in the prow than the poop.

Bear this in mind when you come to cut out the wood or cork. You will find it easier to make the funnel out of a separate piece of wood. When you have painted it, glue it to the deck.

Since every port has more than one tug at its disposal, you can make several to the same design.

Port installations

The installations required by a modern port to cater for all its needs are countless: platforms for open storage, internal roads, railway lines to allow goods trains and container wagons to reach the jetties where ships are moored, special covered warehouses for every kind of goods, cranes, equipment for repairing ships, customs houses . . .

Methods of loading. *Today, there are very many different ways of loading and unloading goods arriving in the port. It is in fact true to say that there is a special system for each kind of merchandise, and quays specially designed for loading and storing it. Within the loading zone of every port, there are quays designed for the traffic in minerals, sugar, gas and oil.*

The central photograph shows the loading zone in a river port. Travelling cranes are lined up along the quays. This kind of crane is highly suitable for unloading goods carried by non-specialised cargo-ships. These goods are usually packed into cases or medium-sized crates. The crane lifts the case by means of a hook attached to its jib and puts it down on the quay. The advantage of these travelling cranes is that they are mounted on rails (as shown in the photograph on the left) and can move along the quay on huge rails to reach the desired spot.

Above right, a floating crane capable of lifting up to 400 tonnes. Its great mobility makes it very useful for unloading ships in difficult places.

Right, loading a container vessel by means of the "roll-on, roll-off" method. According to experts, vessels equipped for this method will be the ships of the future. By this system, the goods are carried into the ship on special lorries and packed in the hold by moving platforms. The advantages of this system are enormous: it shortens the length of time a ship must stay in the port, so reducing berthing fees. Every modern medium-sized port today is equipped with these special quays, built with a ramp running down to the sea and presenting the visitor with a very curious sight indeed.

  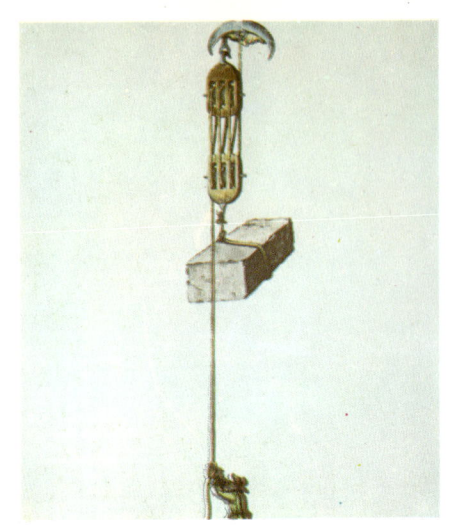

Man discovered the power of the hoist many years ago. Since then, methods of loading and unloading have greatly changed.

The first "modern" cranes are the result of the industrial revolution of the eighteenth and nineteenth centuries. It was then that, with the growth in industry and commerce, it became necessary to build powerful machines for loading and unloading. These machines, which were either stationary or floating, improved the efficiency of such ancient inventions as the pulley and hoist. Later the improvements made on these machines, together with the application of new inventions and the great advances resulting from research on highly resistant materials, gave rise to the impressive and powerful hoists and cranes we see today.

Cranes of yesterday and today. *Above, are three kinds of ancient crane. Although they look primitive, they work on the same mechanical principles as the cranes of today.*

Left, an enormous crane in the Swedish dockyards of Kockums; it is capable of lifting 800 tonnes. In these same dockyards, another crane capable of lifting 1,500 tonnes has just been completed; it may be the most powerful crane in existence.

42

Storage systems. *Just as there are various ways of loading, there are different kinds of storage systems specially devised for each type of merchandise. Above left, the oil port of Ras-Tanura in Saudi Arabia, the most important specialised port in the world. Right, a special silo for storing cement in the port of Bilbao. The photograph below shows a storage area in the container terminal of the port of Le Havre, in France.*

Dry docks. *This is where ships are cleaned and repaired. It is possible to do this only when the submerged part of the hull is lifted clear of the water. Dry docks of the floating variety (right) sink beneath the surface so that the vessel may lodge between its walls. When the ship is in the dock, the water inlets are closed, the water pumped out, and the dock surfaces again.*

Dry docks of the stationary variety are fitted with suction pumps which syphon water out of the dock until the hull of the ship is uncovered. To refloat the boat, the dock is filled with water once again and the vessel towed out.

June, 1944. *The Allies disembarking in Normandy. Some floating jetties have been brought to the coast to allow the military transport ships to moor.*

This harbour contruction was a remarkable demonstration of how far man could go in the search for improving harbour techniques.

Right, a partial view of a breakwater in a harbour. Dykes, groynes and breakwaters are built to check the movement of the waves, protect navigation channels and provide a wide expanse of permanently still water near the harbour.

Loading oil and gas. *Above and below, two views of the new installations in the port of Marseilles, in France. Above, the installations used for loading and storing gas. Gas is carried by sea in tankers – ships specially built for the purpose. Because of the extreme danger involved in carrying this cargo, special kinds of steel are used to build these ships. Endless precautions are also taken when the ship is manoeuvring and while the gas is being transferred to the storage tanks. Below, the quays for loading oil and its by-products. Right, an aerial view of Marseilles harbour, built in the Bay of Fos. The two leading quays are circled.*

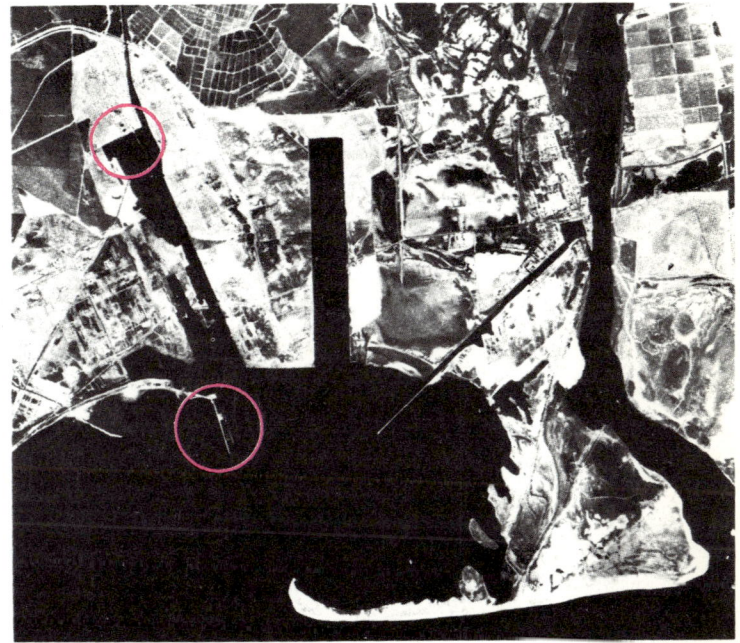

45

How to make cranes for the model

This little crane, which is of a size in proportion to the model, is made out of thin sticks of wood. With these cranes, your harbour can begin its most important and complex function, the traffic in goods.

1. Take two pieces of wood about 2.5cm long and 1cm wide and at the centre cut away an area 7 or 8cm long and 4mm high. Then glue a little stick – a matchstick is suitable – onto each piece of wood as shown in the diagram above.

When these two pieces have been put together as shown in the illustration, glue two sticks of wood about 4.5cm long to each side.

3. Cut two more toothpicks to a length of about 4cm and glue them so that they touch the tips of the sticks you have just glued. Attach a small ring to the point formed by the four sticks. Lastly, place a small piece of balsa wood 1.5×1.5×0.5cm on one side of the crane.

2. Join the two pieces you made as instructed in the last paragraph with two sticks 2.5cm long placed horizontally. To make sure that the crane will be steady, fit it with two other sticks placed diagonally. Then take two toothpicks about 3cm long and glue them to the top, making the tips meet as shown above.

4. While the glue on the crane is drying, cut out a very thin strip of wood about 10cm long.

Make a hole at each end and slide it through the two cavities you made in the upper pieces of the crane. When the strip of wood is in place, pass a thread through the end holes and the ring. The load can be made out of a piece of balsa wood suspended from a length of wire.

47

How to make a lighthouse for the model

MATERIALS
Balsa wood
Felt
Two thin electric wires: one 20cm long
and the other 10cm long
A sheet of tinplate 4cm×1cm
A small switch
Thin cardboard
A round 1.5-volt battery
A bulb for the battery
Glue
Gloss paint
A cotton-reel

TOOLS
A pair of scissors
A screwdriver
Paintbrush

It is essential for a port to have a lighthouse for guiding vessels approaching the entrance at night. Your lighthouse works on a battery. Choose one that is not too large so that the final result will not be out of proportion to the rest of the model.

1. Take two strips of wood 11cm long and 2cm wide and glue them to two other pieces of wood 2cm long and 2cm wide. Paint all this black and leave it to one side for the moment.

This wooden structure should be accurately and firmly glued; if it is not, you will find it difficult to work on. You should therefore use good-quality glue which forms a strong bond.

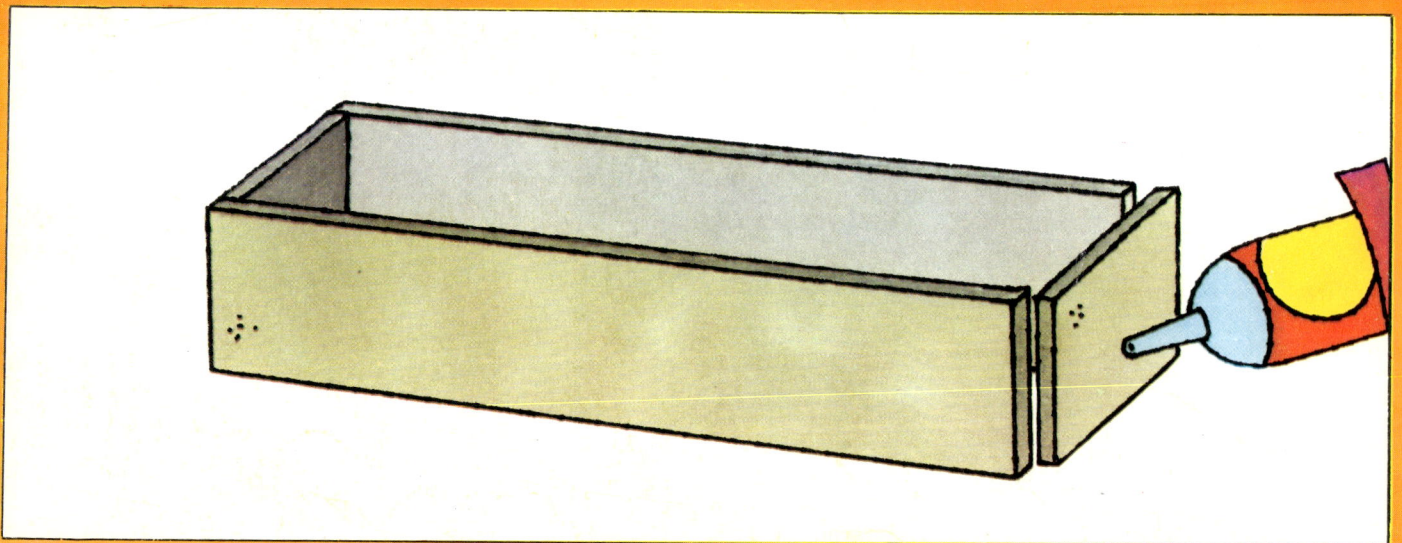

48

2. Separately, take a piece of thin felt, of the same kind as you used for the quays and the road. Draw a band on it 10.5cm long and 2cm wide, adding the shape shown in the drawing on to one end. To reinforce it, glue it onto a piece of cardboard as shown in the illustration below.

3. With a pair of small scissors, make two holes in the strip of felt, one 0.5cm across in the upper end and another 1.5cm across at the other end. When you have made the holes, glue the strip of felt onto the wooden structure you have already made.

4. Now take the switch and the two electric wires. Strip one end of each of the wires and attach them to the switch, taking good care to tighten the screws again.

To connect them, it is not necessary to strip the wires very much; about 1cm is enough.

5. Take the sheet of tinplate 4cm long and 1cm wide. Make a mark 1.5cm from the left-hand edge, another 0.5cm from the last, a third 1cm on, and fourth 0.5cm on. Then bend the tin along these markings, giving it the shape shown in the illustra-tion. When you have bent it, make a small hole in the longest end and attach the short wire, which should already be connected to the switch. Attach it as carefully as you can because if it came undone the lighthouse would stop working.

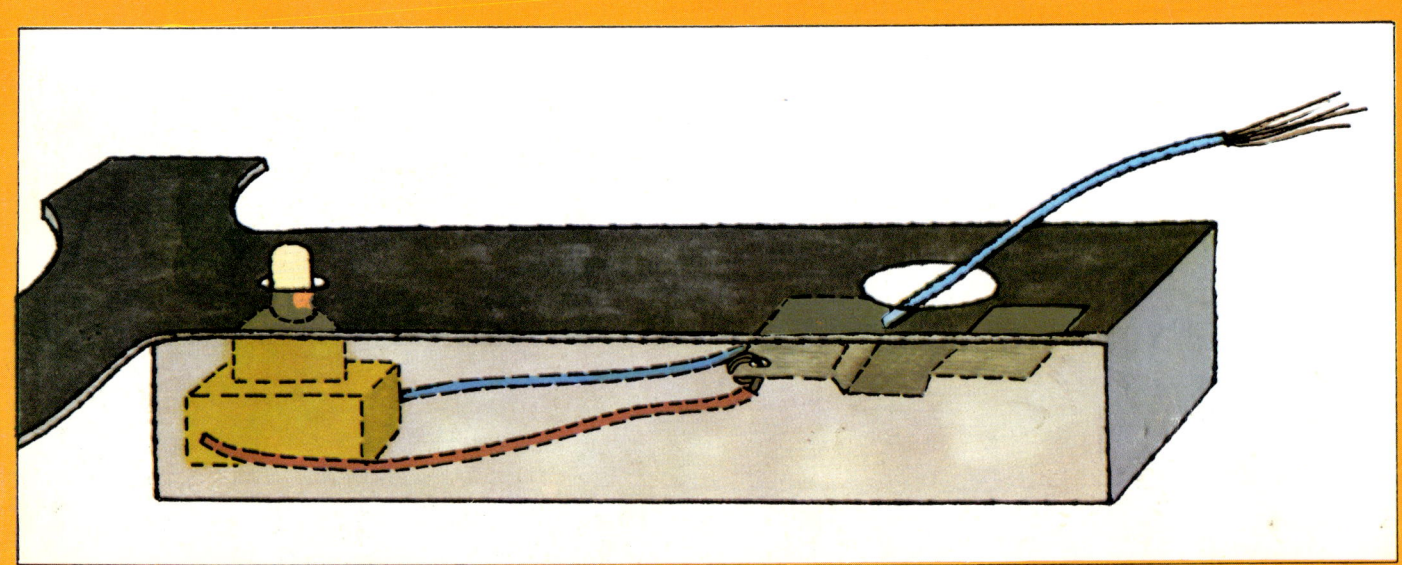

6. Place the switch inside the wooden structure so that the button sticks up out of the small hole in the felt. Thread the blue wire through the large hole at the other end, then glue the tinplate onto the cardboard beneath the felt. When you glue the tinplate, make sure that the sunken part lies directly beneath the large hole in the felt as shown on the diagram above.

7. Take the inside of a cotton-reel and place it over the large hole, passing the blue wire through the centre of it. If the inside of the cotton-reel is too narrow, make a cardboard cylinder of the right size. When you have pushed the cylinder or cotton-reel into the hole, secure it with glue.

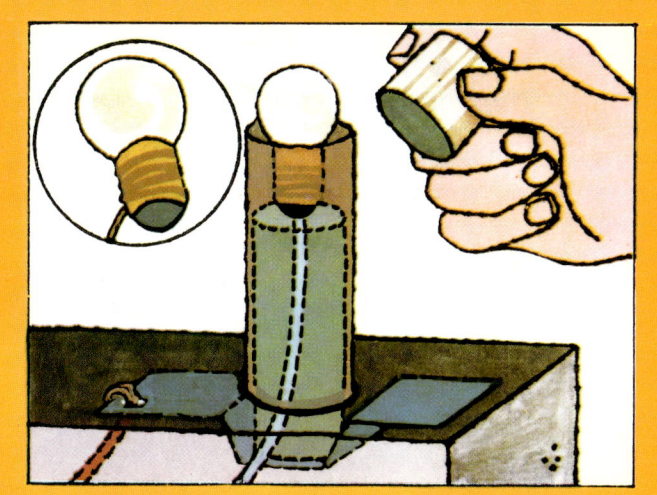

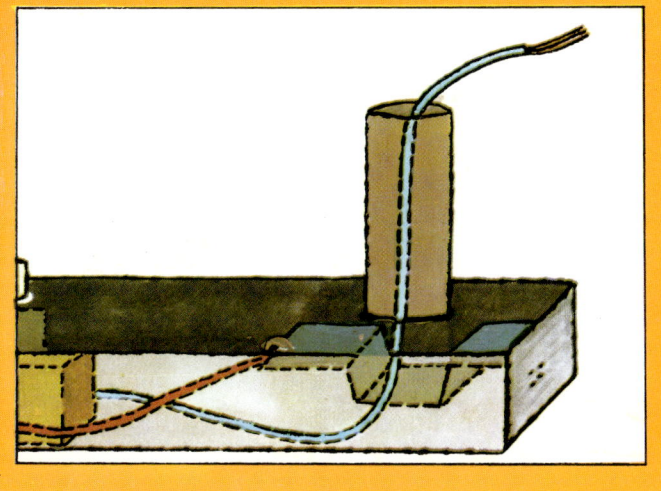

8. Place a small 1.5-volt battery in the cylinder, making sure that the bottom end touches the tin plate. Then take the wire sticking out of the cylinder and wind it round the socket of the light bulb. Lastly, place the bulb in the cylinder and push it down until it touches the battery.

Place the cranes you have made on the loading quays, as shown in the illustration below. You can make as many as you like and move them wherever you want. The lighthouse of the

model has been placed at the entrance to the harbour with the ramp resting on and glued to the ground. Take special note of the position of the switch.

A. Container berth
B. Ferry berth
C. Cargo and tanker berth
D. Fishing harbour
E. Landing stage for sailing boats

1. Harbour lighthouse
2. Cranes for containers
3. Port headquarters
4. Silos and warehouses
5. Tugs and lifeboats
6. Red Cross
7. Swivel bridge
8. Barges
9. Fishing village
10. Sailing club
11. Pilot's launch
12. Buoys and beacons

Different kinds of ships

"Specialised" ships. *Nowadays, ships are used for other purposes besides those involving the transport of goods or carrying passengers.*

Right, the Lenin, *the world's first automatic ice-breaker. It can cut through layers of ice up to two metres thick; its job is to keep a passage open for Soviet cargo ships sailing along the Siberian coast. The photograph below shows a ship fitted out for space research; it could almost be called a floating space laboratory.*

MOBIL PEGASUS
LONDON

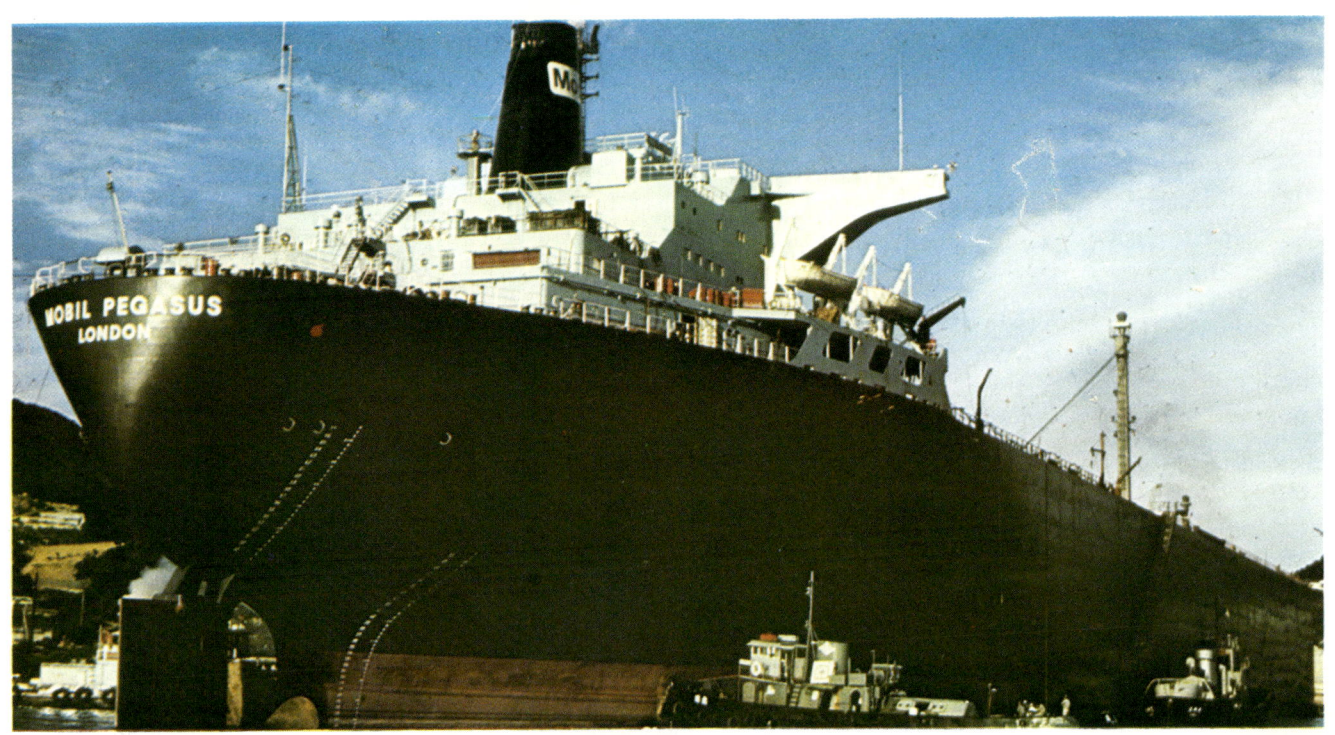

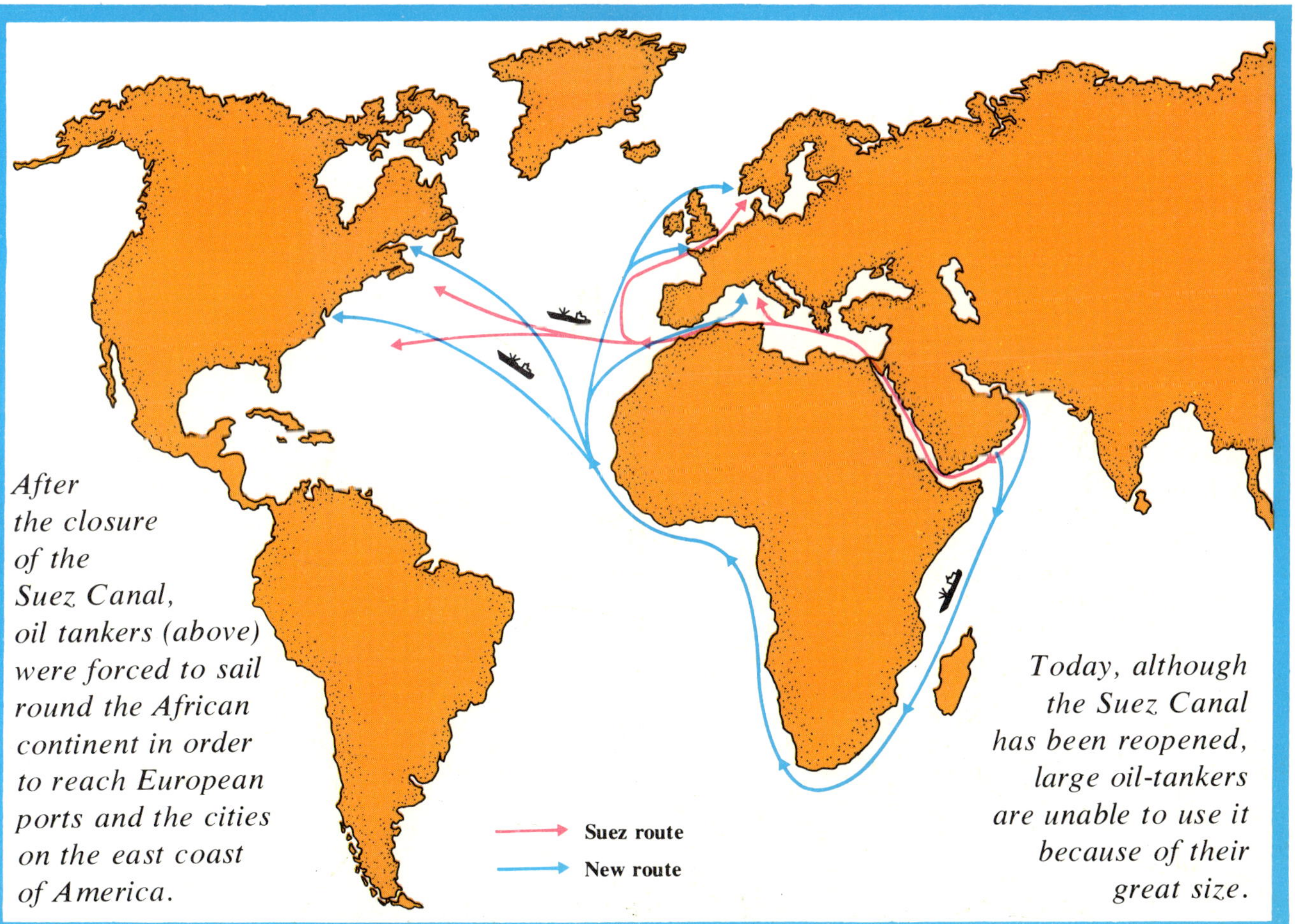
Suez route
New route

After the closure of the Suez Canal, oil tankers (above) were forced to sail round the African continent in order to reach European ports and the cities on the east coast of America.

Today, although the Suez Canal has been reopened, large oil-tankers are unable to use it because of their great size.

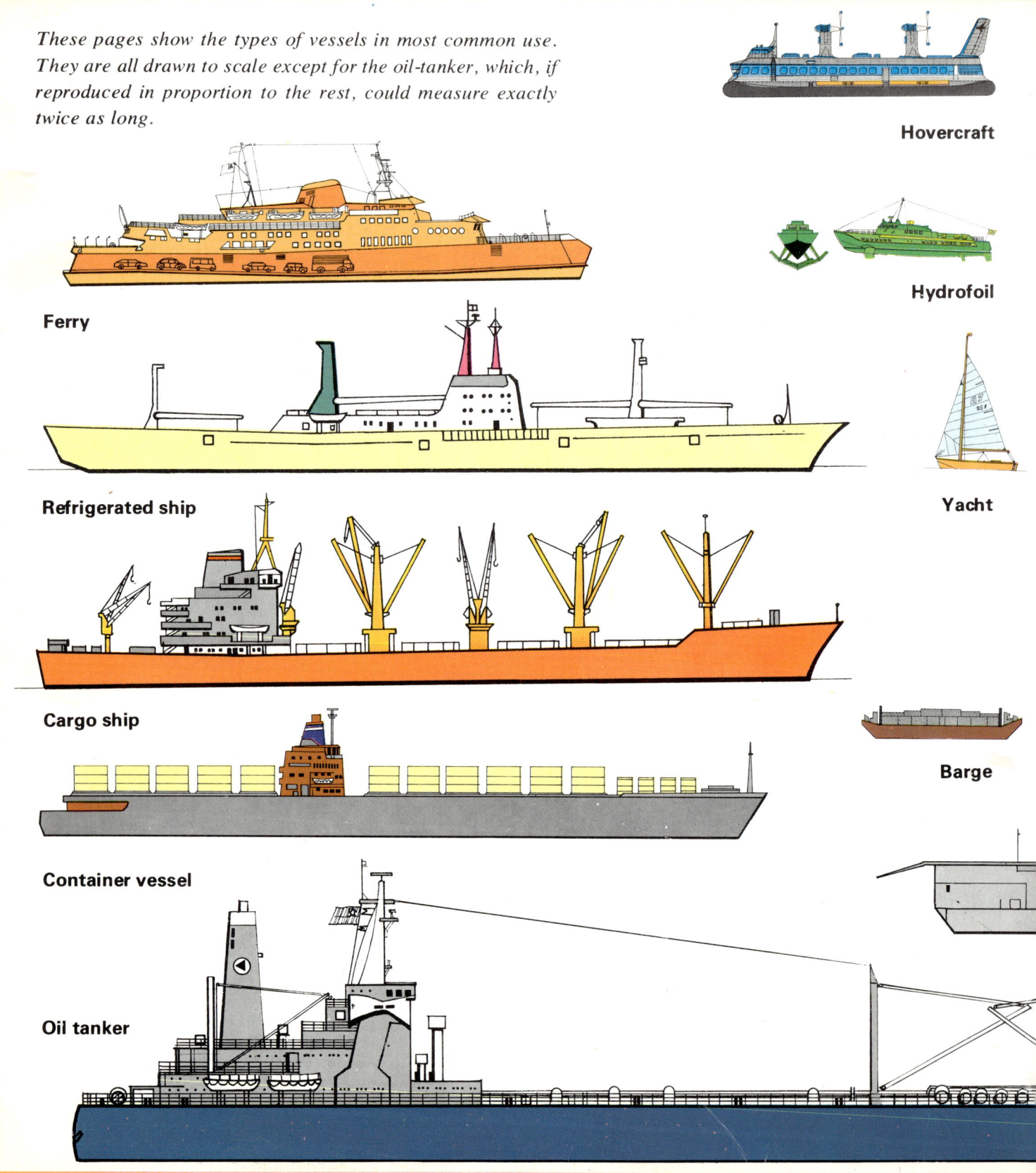

These pages show the types of vessels in most common use. They are all drawn to scale except for the oil-tanker, which, if reproduced in proportion to the rest, could measure exactly twice as long.

Hovercraft

Ferry

Hydrofoil

Refrigerated ship

Yacht

Cargo ship

Barge

Container vessel

Oil tanker

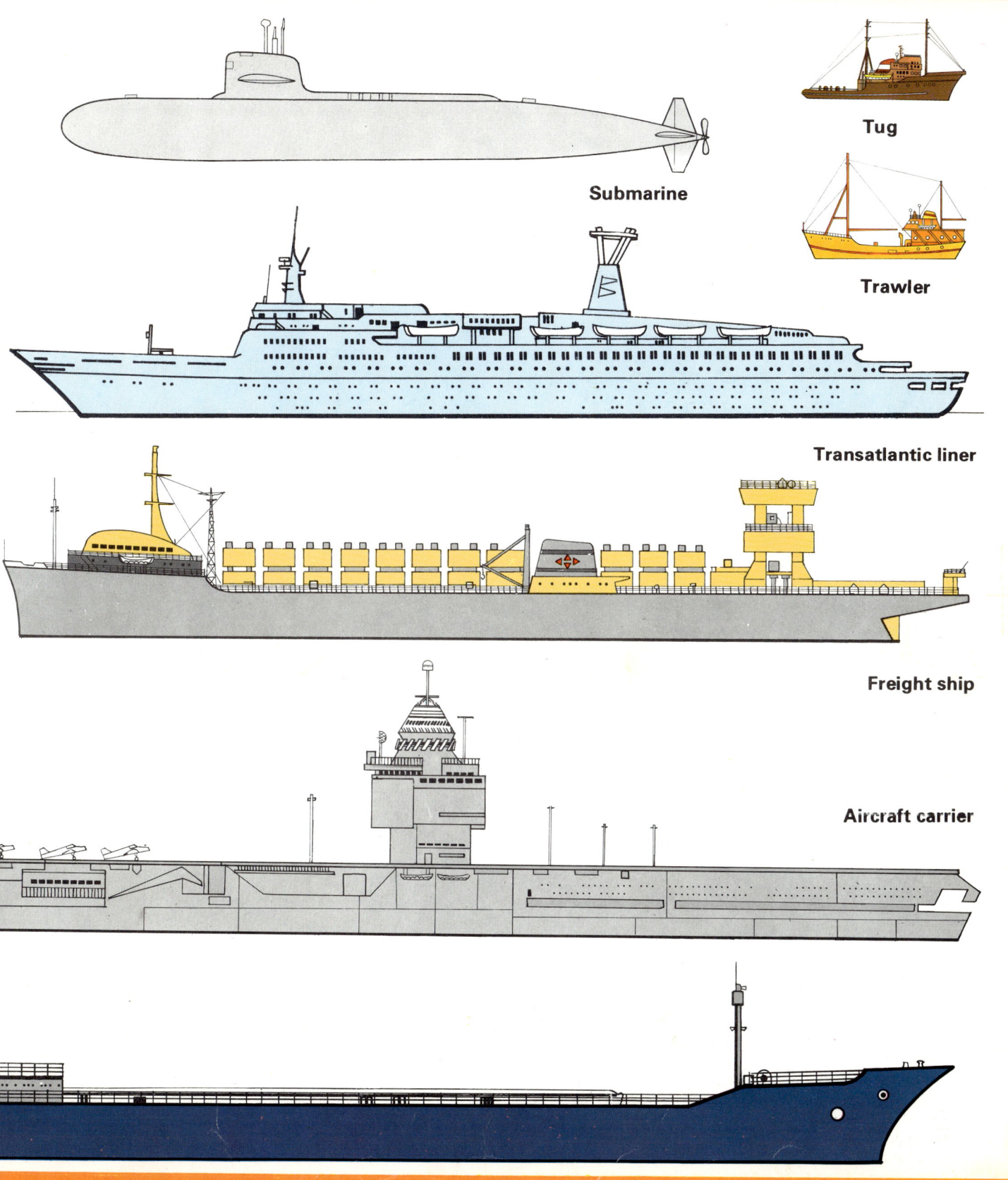

Submarine

Tug

Trawler

Transatlantic liner

Freight ship

Aircraft carrier

How to make
a lorry

MATERIALS
  Glue
  Gloss paint of different colours
  A block of balsa wood 7.5×8×5cm
  Plywood
  Two steel rods
  Four wheels taken from an old toy car
  Four rivets for the wheels
  Two red drawing-pins

TOOLS
  A saw
  Nails
  A hammer
  Paintbrushes
  A gimlet

You will be able to use this lorry for carrying the goods unloaded by crane from the ships or from any other model of yours. The next chapter explains how to make a crane.

1. Cut two bars of plywood 24cm long and 2cm wide. Then take a gimlet and make two holes in the wood. It is important to make the holes at the same height in each bar so that the axles for the wheels will slide through easily, as shown in the illustration below.

2. Take a block of balsa wood and cut two notches 4cm long, 2cm wide and 0.5cm deep in the underside. Take the bars that you have just cut out and glue them in each of the notches. To make them firm, hammer in some long thin nails. Coat all this in gloss paint and leave it to dry.

3.   Take a sheet of plywood and cut it into four pieces having the following measurements: two pieces 20.5×3cm; one 8×3cm and another 8×20cm. Put together with thin nails, these pieces will form the back of the lorry. Paint this part any colour you like.

4.   When the paint on the back of the lorry is dry, glue it onto the wooden bars, then secure it with nails. Remember that the back of the lorry should be positioned a little way back from the cab, as shown in the illustration below.

5.   Slide the steel bars through the holes in the bars; these will be the lorry's axles. Push the four wheels onto them.

6.   Paint in the cab windows, push the two red drawing-pins and the silver rivets in at the front, and your lorry is finished.

How to make a crane

MATERIALS
Two blocks of balsa wood 15×4.5×10.5cm
Two sheets of plastic of the same size
Two bars of wood 30×3×1cm
Three bars of wood 33×2×1cm
Four blocks of balsa wood 2.5×2×2cm and two blocks 2×1×1cm
A sheet of aluminium 5×6cm
A piece of balsa wood 8×8×1cm
Thin string
Paint
A metal hook
Some eye-screws
The key from a sardine-tin

TOOLS
A saw
Paintbrush
A gimlet
A penknife
Nails
A hammer
a hacksaw

The structure of this crane is based on two important things: the movement of the two bars forming the jib and the accurate positioning of the two black bars supporting them.

1. Glue two sheets of plastic onto each block of balsa wood so that when they are brought together, they will turn smoothly. Cut four blocks of wood 2.5×2×2cm and glue them on the four corners of the lower block. Paint this piece and leave it to dry.

2. Paint the two 30×3cm bars of wood black. Make a peg about 3cm long at one end of each of the bars. To do this, cut away the wood to a length of 3cm from the end and smooth the peg with sandpaper, as shown, right.

3. Take a drill or gimlet and bore two holes about 2.5cm apart in the upper block forming the base. Push the black bars into the holes and secure them with strong glue. When in place, the bars will stand about 1cm apart. Glue a small piece of wood to their upper end.

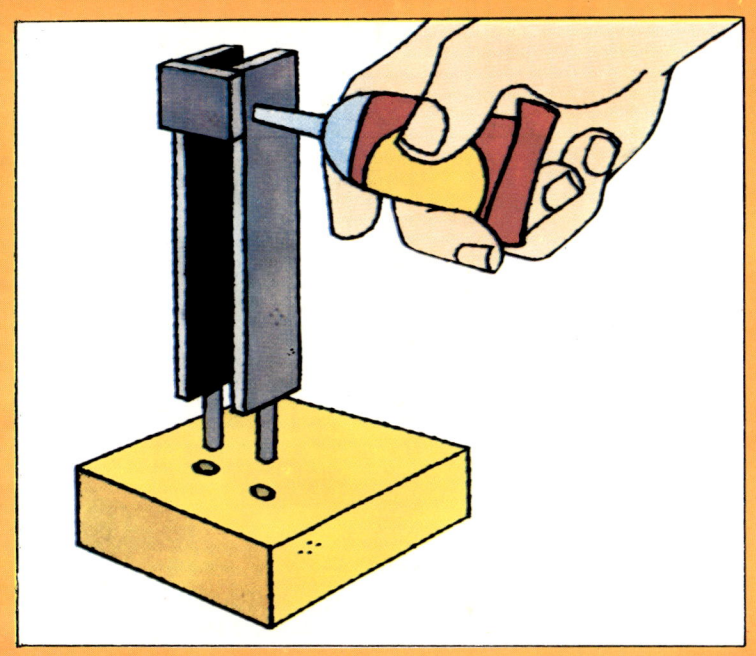

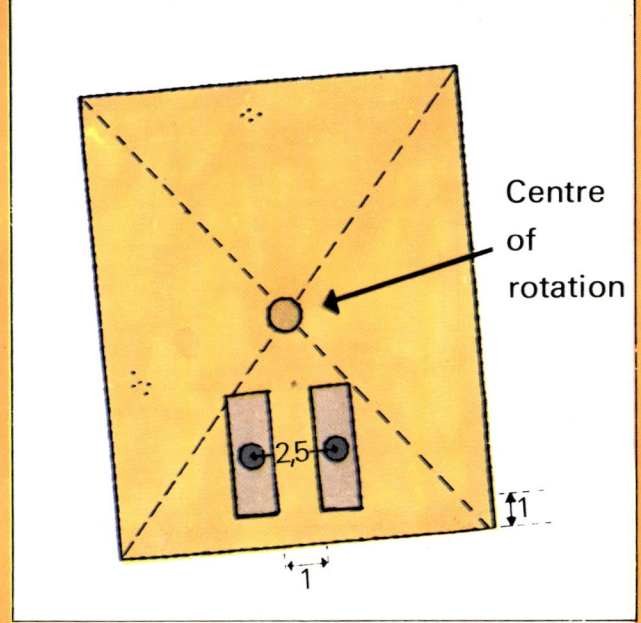

Centre of rotation

4. Take a white pencil and on a sheet of aluminium measuring 5×6cm, draw pieces A and B, following the measurements given in the illust- ration. Then cut them both out with a hacksaw, bore the holes and bend the pieces as shown in the illustration below.

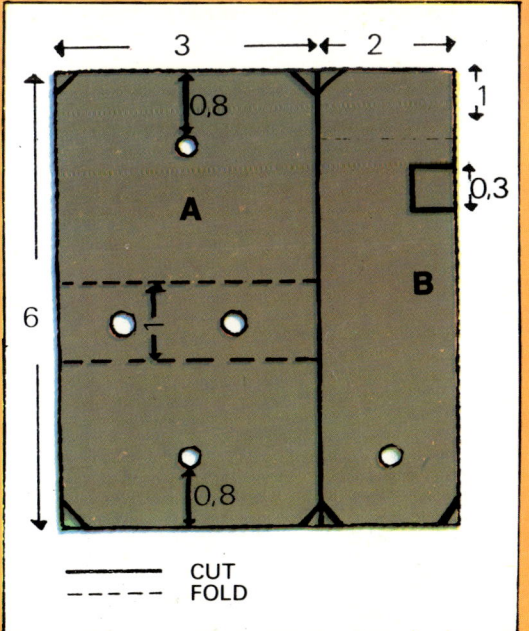

CUT
FOLD

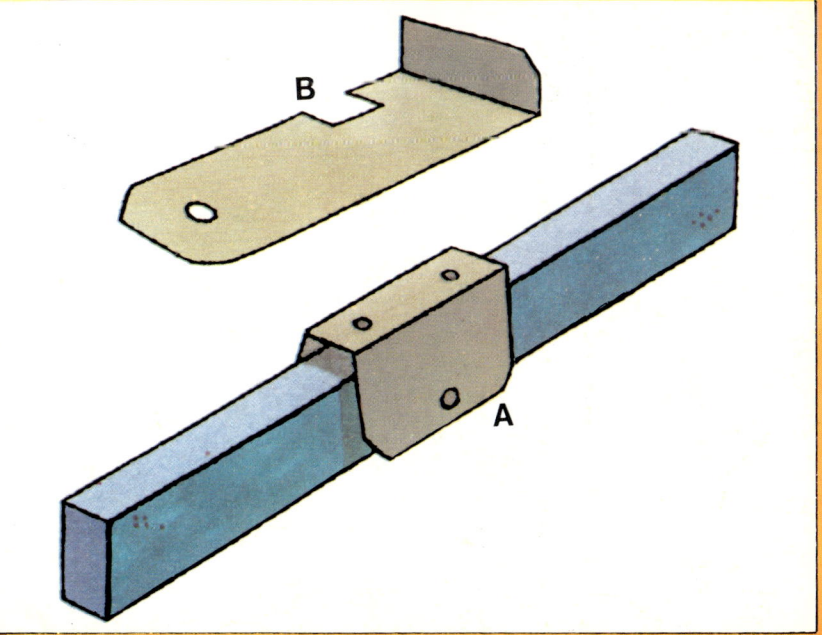

15

3,5

Centre of
rotation

5. Nail the piece of aluminium A onto the upper block of the base. Hammer an 8-cm nail into one of the holes; this will be the crane's axis of rotation. Push in another, smaller nail to fix the aluminium firmly to the wood. Then take three bars of wood 33cm long and make holes in them as shown in the illustration.

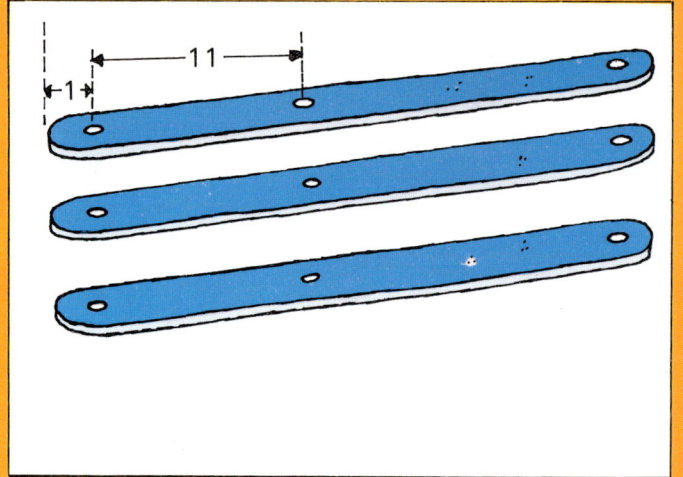

11

1

6. Join these three bars with a nail about 3.5cm long pushed through the holes at one end. Then flatten the point of the nail. Do this by holding the three joined bars on the floor and tapping the point with a hammer until it is bent over or flattened against the wood.

Cut out a small block of balsa wood and glue it to the lower end of the middle bar. But do this only after you have attached the jib to the black bars.

11

7. Take the 30-cm bar and fix it between the two bars of the jib by passing nails through the holes made 11cm from the end. Firmly push two eye-screws into the end of the 30-cm bar so that one leans to the left and the other to the right. These screws will take the string of the crane.

Here, too, you should fix the bar with a 3.5-cm nail and then flatten the point. Although not the most difficult, this step is perhaps the most important in putting the crane together. See that the four bars move easily on their axes and take care that the screws do not hinder the movement of the crane.

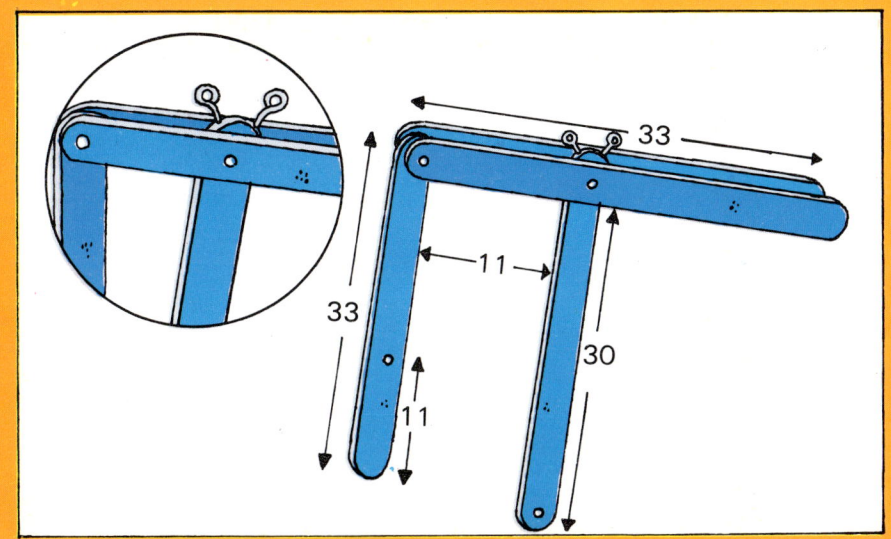

8. Between the two ends of the upper part of the jib, slide in a round block of wood with an eye-screw pushed into it. Fix this piece with a nail pushed through the holes you made in the jib. You could also use a sewing-machine bobbin with a small piece of wood nailed in above it to keep the string in place. look closely at the illustration below to ensure that you get this stage right

63

9. The string is wound round a crank made out of the key of a sardine-tin. Slide the crank through the holes in the black bars; these should be made about 3.5cm above the base. Then bend the crank at one end as shown in the drawing.

To make it easier to load and unload cargo later on, make a platform 8×8cm square. Bore holes in the four corners and thread string through them for the platform to hang from.

This platform is not for use on all occasions, as you will sometimes be loading cases tied with string and hanging directly from the hook as shown in the photograph at bottom of page 65.

10. To lock the crank whenever you want to, nail the piece of aluminium you have already made onto the outside of the black bar. This piece is moveable and will lock the crank with its notch.

If you want to make the locking action more secure, cut a notch in the handle exactly where the piece of aluminium touches it.

Instead of using the key of a sardine-tin, you could also adapt a metal rod; bent in the right way, this would make just as good a crank.

It is now time to join the jib to the black bars as shown in the final photograph.

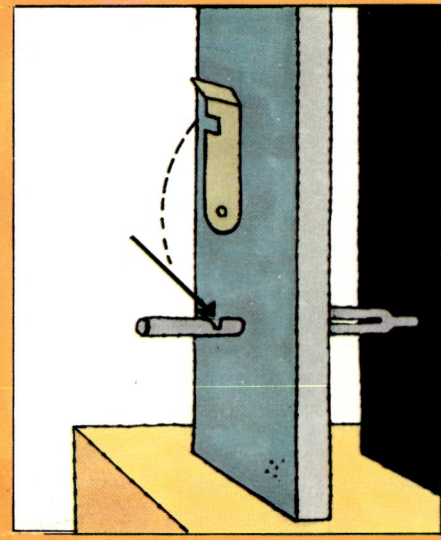

11.   You can now wind the string round the crank and thread it through the screws in the central bar and end bobbin. Tie a hook to the end of the string and hang the loading platform onto it.

As you will sometimes have to lock the jib in a certain position, attach a small catch to the block of wood acting as a counterweight and push four or five short nails into the black bar, positioning them within the reach of the catch.

In this way you will be able to vary the angle of the jib according to the proximity of the cargo.

When problems arise

Shipwrecks near the coast. *In the past, when a vessel was in process of sinking, attempts were made to save the crew by sending a cable from the beach out towards the ship by means of a cannon. The men would then pull themselves up to the beach on the cable which was attached to a winch on the shore.*

Is sailing dangerous today?

The days when putting out to sea was a whole adventure have passed into history. Sailors today no longer have to rely upon their own resources or trust to good luck.

Nowadays, the likelihood of accidents occurring is very remote. The sea claims very few lives now, but, even so, when a ship's radio receives an S.O.S. from another vessel in difficulties there are some moments of anguish as tense as in days gone by.

Coastguard vessels. *These are medium-sized craft which are very light and are fitted with excellent radio equipment. They are in permanent contact with the harbour-master's office and keep it informed of any problems that arise within the territorial waters they are responsible for patrolling.*

The risk of being shipwrecked is also remote. The very structure of large ships is designed to remove this danger or at least to stop the vessel from sinking rapidly. The different sections of a ship are separated by thick metal walls and linked by doors which seal tightly when they close, thus isolating one section from another. Thanks to this system of separate compartments, the ship will not necessarily sink even if she is taking in water.

But it is chiefly the systems of communication by radio that have made the most valuable contribution to safety at sea.

Salvage and health. *Above, a group of frogmen returning from a salvage operation. Their job is to dredge the sea-bed, recover sunken vessels and sometimes bring up the bodies of people who have drowned. Left, a port's medical launch. No ship is allowed to moor at the quays until the state of health of its crew members has been ascertained.*

Damage. *The tugs are the first to come to the aid of damaged ships, which are then towed to the repair docks. Rescuing a ship in distress on the high seas can be very dangerous. This task is carried out by special tugs which are crewed by highly skilled sailors.*

The oil slick. *This is the modern scourge of seas and beaches. When a tanker catches fire, goes aground or collides with another tanker, oil spews out into the sea. Right, a semi-submerged oil-tanker.*

Some modern vessels carry various devices which, in case of accidents, can be used to avert total disaster: for example, fire-hoses fitted to the vessel which suck up sea-water and spray it onto the flames. But not all ships are suited to this method of fire fighting. Oil-tankers and ships carrying certain chemical substances deal with fires breaking out on board with foam or sand sprayed under pressure. Water might only increase the flames.

In addition to the ship's own equipment, ports also rely on teams of people and fleets of fire-fighting launches.

Fires. When fire breaks out in the harbour or its immediate surroundings and the ship's cargo presents no threat, all the harbour's fire-fighting teams go into action. If, on the other hand, the cargo carried by the ship is dangerous (explosives, inflammable gases, for example) the crew is evacuated and the ship blown up in the open sea.

How to make a large lighthouse

The only trouble you are likely to have in building this lighthouse involves setting up the wires and connecting them to the electric plug, the switch and the bulb. If you find you need help, ask a knowledgeable adult for assistance with this part.

1.   Find a cardboard tube of the kind used for storing plans and posters. Cut it down to a height of about 25cm and cut the holes for the windows at different levels and make the doorway. Keep the piece of cardboard you have cut from the doorway.

Cut a disc out of thick cardboard measuring about 14cm in diameter. Make one hole in the centre of the disc and eight small holes round the edge to allow cold air to pass through to the upper part of the lighthouse. When you have done all this, glue the disc onto the cylinder.

70

2. Take an electric wire about 2m long and thread one end through the centre hole you have just made.

Connect this wire to the socket of a small electric bulb. Connect it as follows: strip the two threads of the wire with a penknife and attach them to the socket, each one with its corresponding screw. Then put a little glue on the base of the socket and fix it over the central hole.

Ask an adult to help you with this stage and all the others involving the electrical installations.

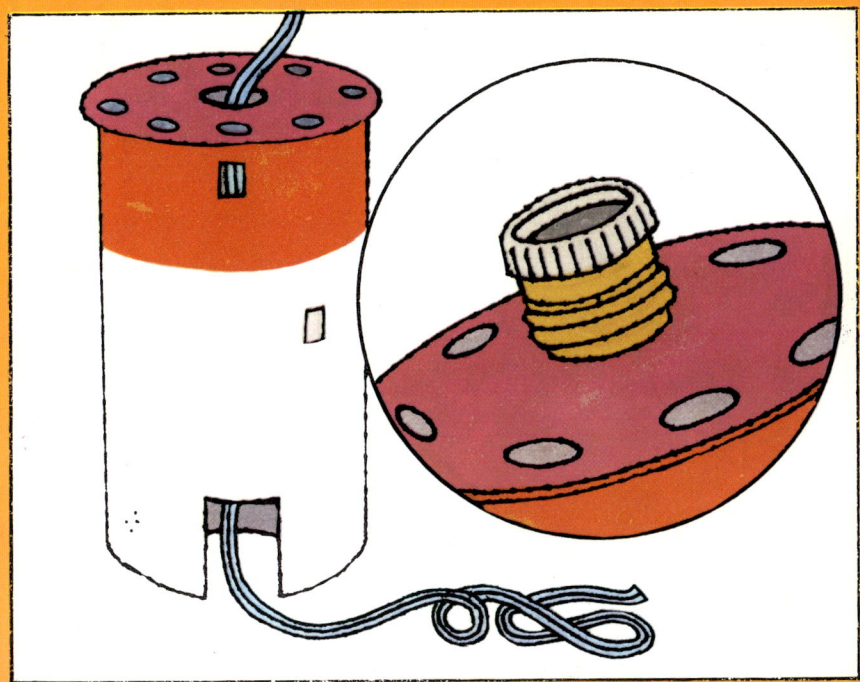

3. Now take the wire and cut one thread only about 30cm from the end connected to the socket. Strip the two separated ends and connect them to the switch, attaching each thread to each of the two screws. Wrap the wires and the switch in insulating tape as shown below.

4. Cut a small notch in the cardboard cylinder forming the tower so that the wire can pass through. Cut a notch at the back of the tower. Pass the wire through the notch, leaving the switch inside, then glue the tower onto a wooden base 20cm long, 13cm wide and 2cm thick.

When you cut the notch, be careful to make it large enough, so that the wire is not trapped when you come to glue the tower onto the wooden base.

If the notch were too small, the wire would eventually become worn and you would have to take the whole thing to pieces to put it right.

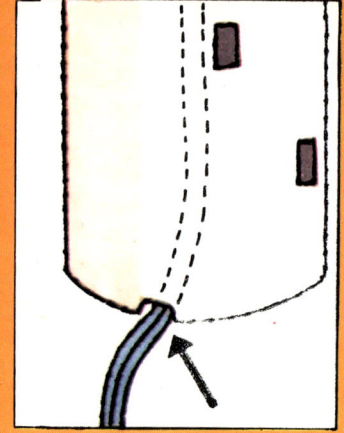 

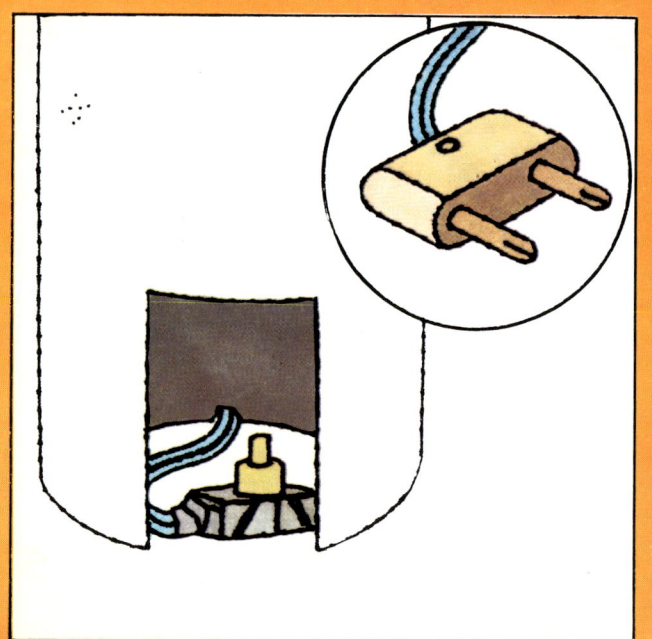

5. When the glue has dried, stick the switch to the wooden base supporting the tower, making sure that the switch stays inside it.

If you like, you can paint the insulating tape covering the switch in black or grey.

Then attach a plug to the end of the wire, pushing the threads though the holes and winding them round the screws.

6. To make the door, take the piece of cardboard you cut out of the cylinder and attach it to the doorway of the tower with sticky tape.

The tape should be wide enough to join the door to the cylinder easily. First stick one half of the tape to the cylinder, then attach the door to the other half, leaving a few millimetres in between to allow the door to open and close.

Adhesive tape

7.   You have already finished the lower part of the lighthouse.

Before going any further, paint the lighthouse and wait for it to dry. Paint the wooden base as well and glue some pebbles to it to give the impression of rocks.

Here, as elsewhere in this book, the colours we used for painting the lighthouse were only chosen as a suggestion. Although lighthouses are in fact usually white and black, or white and red, paint yours in any colours you like.

8.   Cut a strip of white cardboard 23cm long and 8cm high.

Draw a parallel line 1cm above the base. Make small cuts with a pair of scissors along the length of this edge.

Fold the cardboard along the line you drew. This fringe will be the base for the roof of the rotating cap.

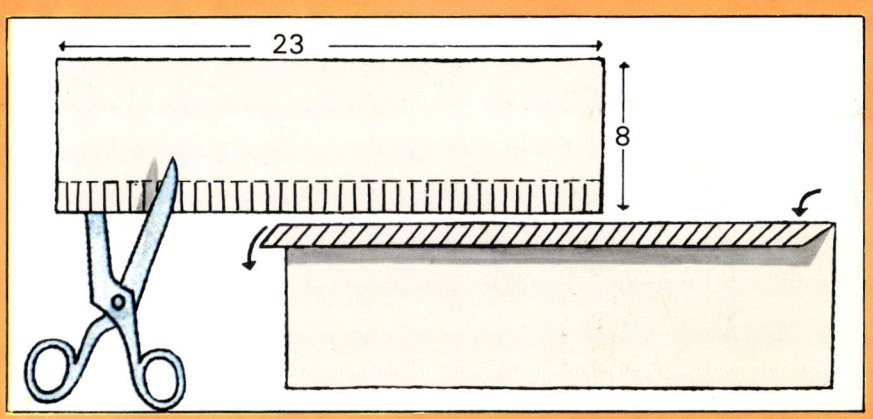

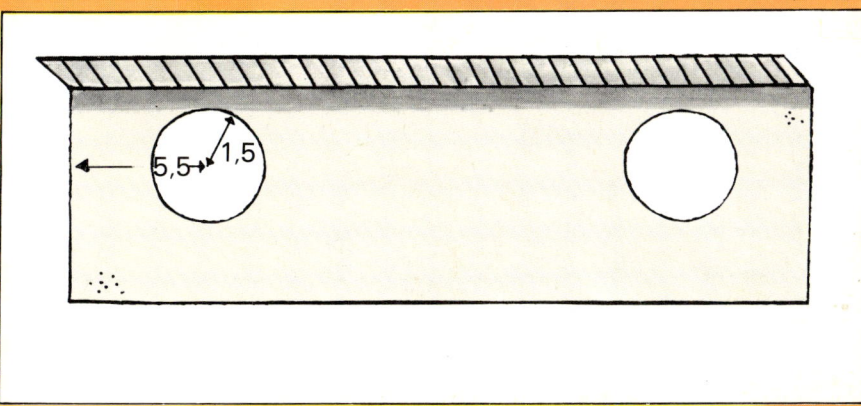

9.   Take a pair of compasses and draw two circles having a radius of 1.5cm on the lower part of the strip of cardboard. The centres of the circles should be 5.5cm away from the sides of the cardboard.

73

10. Next, cut out the two circles by running a penknife along the circumference.

Take two pieces of cellophane paper or plastic and glue them on the inside of the cardboard and behind the holes you have just made. Then join the two edges of the cardboard to make a cylinder. The diagram below shows you what the finished cylinder looks like. Leave it to dry.

11. This step is very important for the smooth operation of the lighthouse. Take every care, therefore, while carrying it out.

On a piece of thin cardboard, draw a circle with a radius of 3.5cm and cut it out. When you have done this, draw another small circle at the centre with a radius of 0.5cm. With a blade, make about eight cuts from the centre outwards.

Gently push the tongues upwards, as shown in the diagram, at the centre of the disc. Glue a piece of rounded glass, which can be taken from a broken light-bulb, inside this "hillock". Take good care to glue the glass in the exact centre of the disc.

12. Midway between the edge and the centre of the disc, draw a rectangle 1×0.5cm and cut it with a penknife on only three of its sides. Push this tab upwards. This "window" will allow the warm air generated by the light-bulb (this will be explained later on) to rise and turn the cap.

To reinforce the window, glue a second, slightly larger, cardboard rectangle onto the tab.

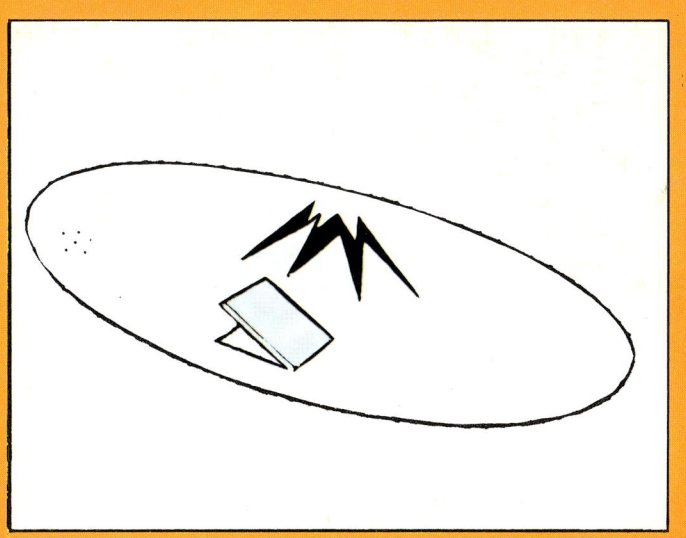

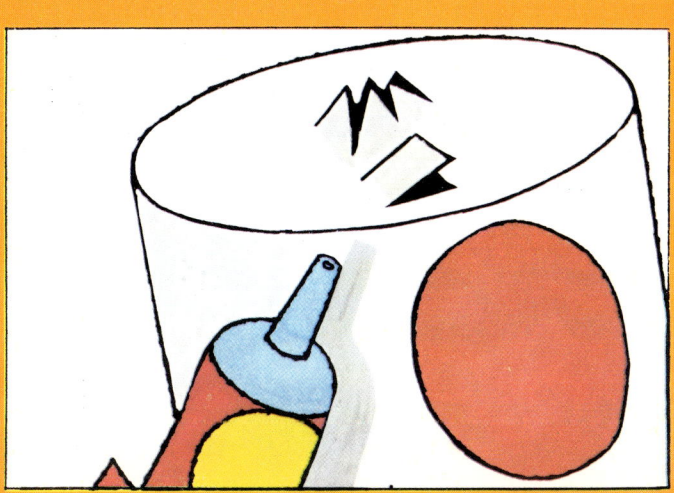

13. Glue the finished disc onto the cardboard cylinder that you have already made. Coat the tongues with glue and make sure that the two pieces are perfectly glued together. Air must pass through the "window" in the disc and nowhere else. The working of the lighthouse depends on the correct construction of this cylinder; you must therefore make it with great care.

14. Buy a small, round, 25-watt light-bulb and screw it into the socket you already have. On top of it and exactly in the centre, glue a drawing-pin upside down. It is essential that the glue you use here is resistant to high temperatures. When the cap is balanced on the point of the drawing-pin, the warm air rising from the lighted bulb will make it rotate.

15. Cut out a strip of white cardboard 30cm long and 10cm wide. Draw four windows in it 3cm wide and 8cm high as shown in the illustration and cut them out.

Then cut out four small pieces of cardboard 1.5cm wide for use as supports and glue them to the spaces in between each window.

Cut four more supports of the same size and glue them to the other side. Then glue each end of the cardboard together to make a cylinder.

The supports you have just glued are important because they allow the air to pass through in order to rotate the cap.

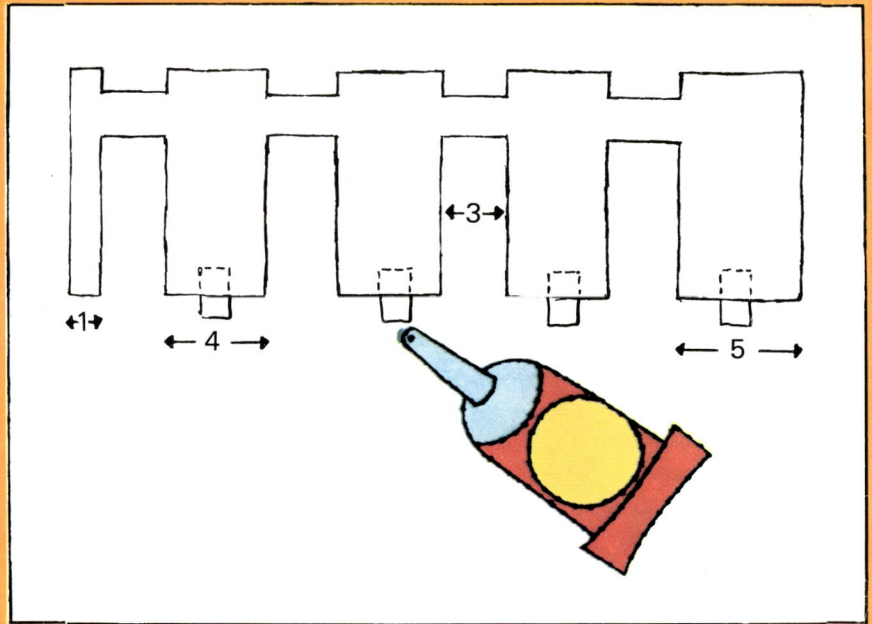

16. On a piece of red cardboard, draw a circle with a radius of 4cm and cut it out. Using the same centre, draw another circle with a radius of 1cm and make a series of cuts, forming a star shape just as you did for the black cap. The diagram below shows what is required.

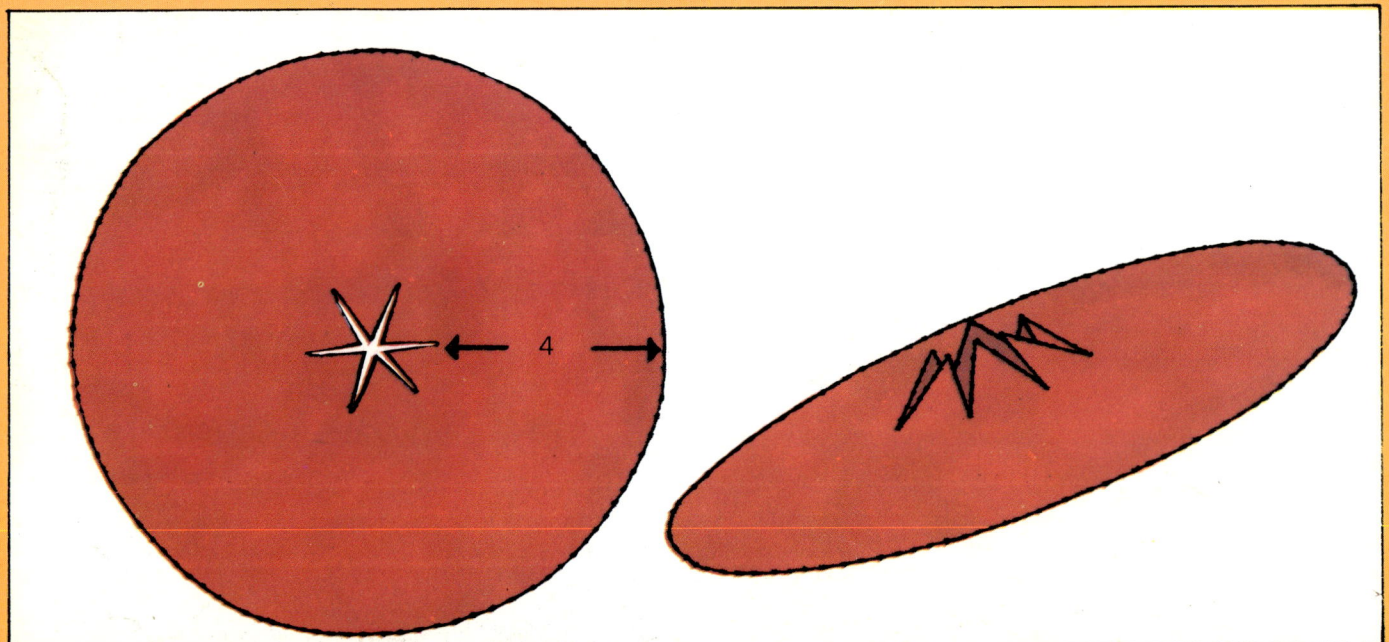

17. Make a cut in the red disc from the outside in and glue one edge onto the other to make a cone.

18. Lastly, cut a strip of plastic netting and glue or push it in round the base of the ledge to make railings.

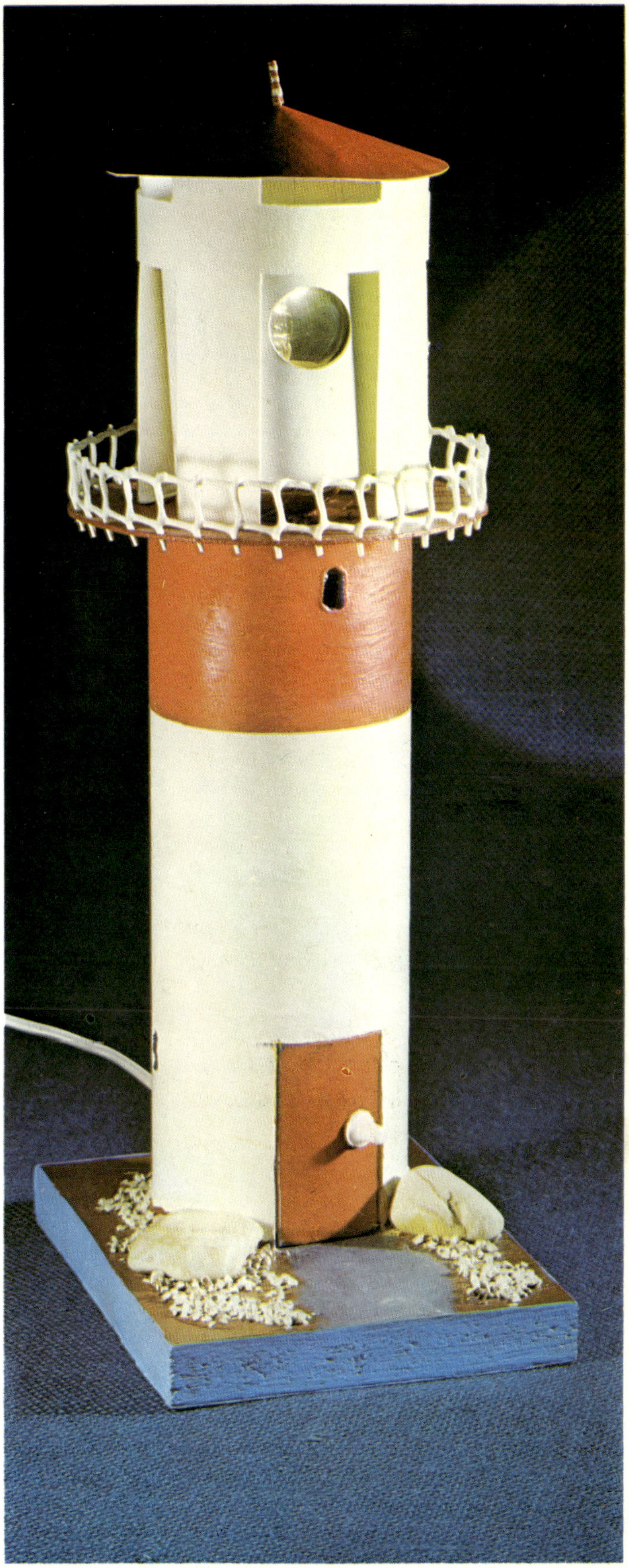

77

How to make the signal flags

These two flags, one red and the other blue (the only colours used for signalling between ships), are made out of two medium-sized pieces of material glued or sewn to a stick. With them, you will be able to communicate with anyone standing at any distance within sight of you.

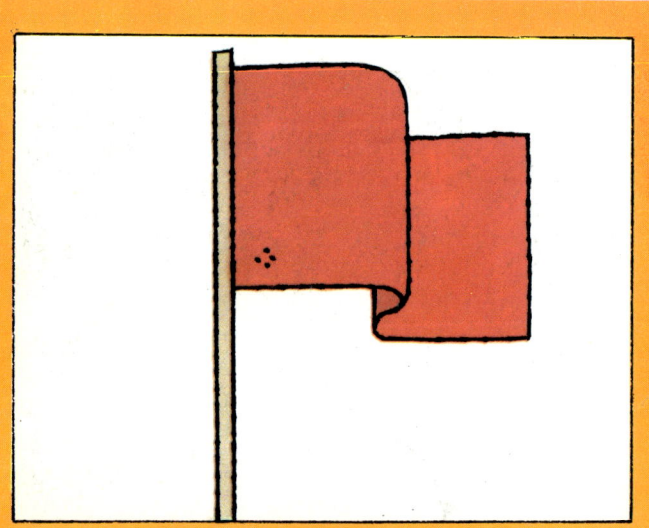

1.   First paint the two sticks white and leave them to dry. Then take a piece of red material about 50×20cm. If it begins to fray when you cut it, make a small hem and tack it with staples if you do not want to sew it.

2.   The procedure for making the second flag is exactly the same as for the first except that the material must be blue. When the paint on the sticks is quite dry, take the pieces of material and attach them by coating the sticks with glue.

Signalling with flags is one of the ways sailors communicate across a certain distance. By holding the flags in different positions, it is possible to signal every letter of the alphabet and send messages from one ship to another. But this must not be confused with the international code of signals, which involves the use of flags bearing different markings; each marking corresponds to a letter, and the flags are placed in the highest possible position to be within the sight of ships.

For the volume of cargo handled there, this is the world's second largest commercial port after Rotterdam. From the Narrows all along the coast of New Jersey, Manhattan and Long Island, the pattern of quays arranged in parallel fashion gives this city, named the Gateway to America, a unique appearance.

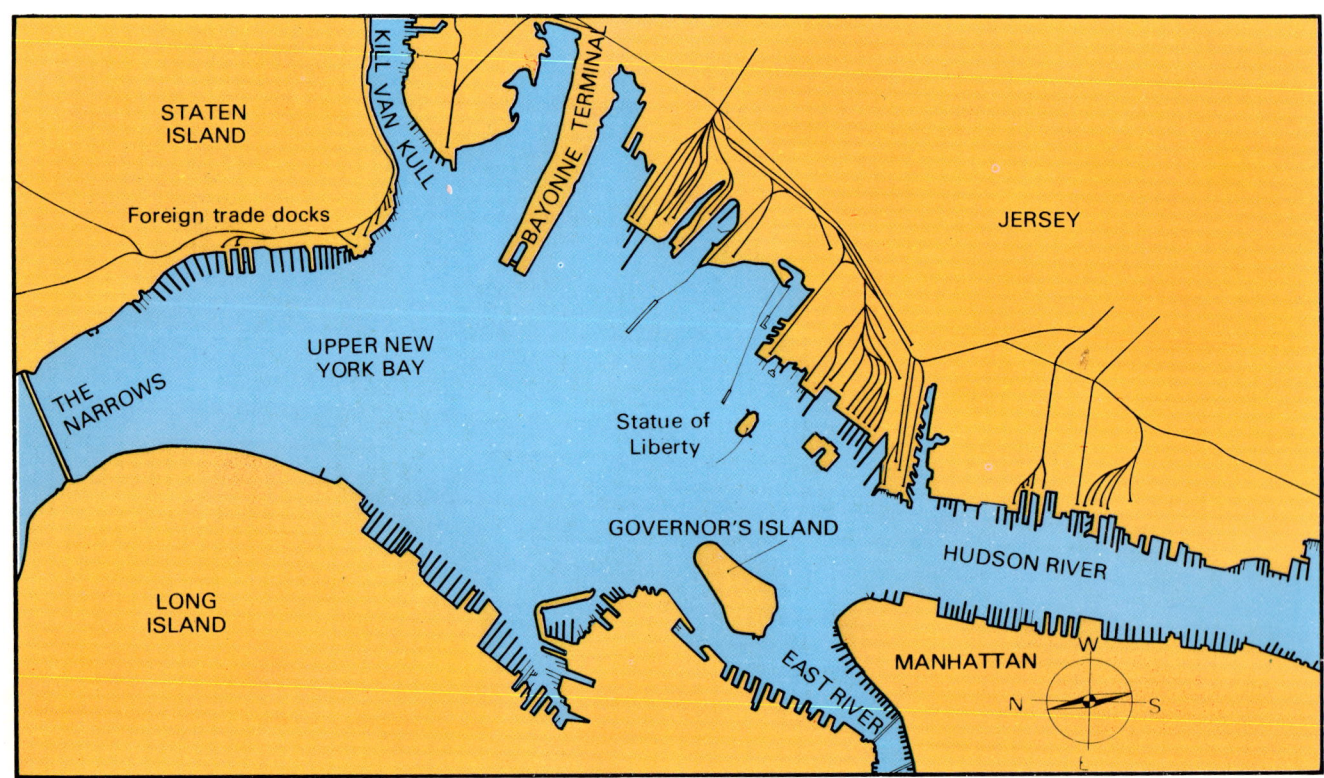

STATEN ISLAND

Foreign trade docks

KILL VAN KULL

BAYONNE TERMINAL

JERSEY

UPPER NEW YORK BAY

THE NARROWS

Statue of Liberty

GOVERNOR'S ISLAND

HUDSON RIVER

LONG ISLAND

EAST RIVER

MANHATTAN

The large number of ships coming to berth there makes it one of the largest ports in the Pacific Ocean. It is also Australia's principal port. Its natural features may be considered to be the best in the world; sheltered by high cliffs, its entrance channel may be used by any kind of ship however deep its draught.

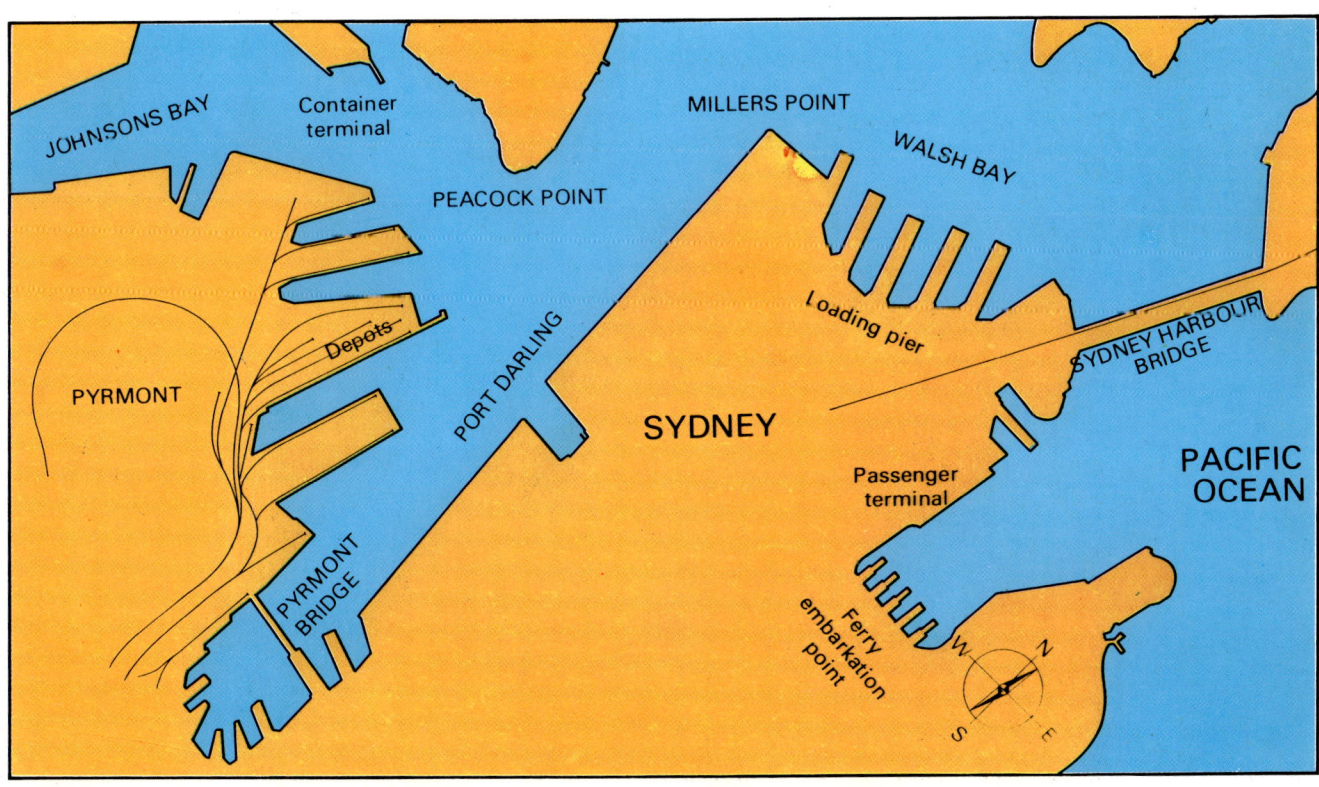

Situated on the banks of the Escaut, it is the second largest port in Europe. Although the depth of its navigation channels reaches eight metres – thirteen metres at high tide – Antwerp is today facing serious technical problems due to the increase in the draught of vessels. Constant dredging is required.

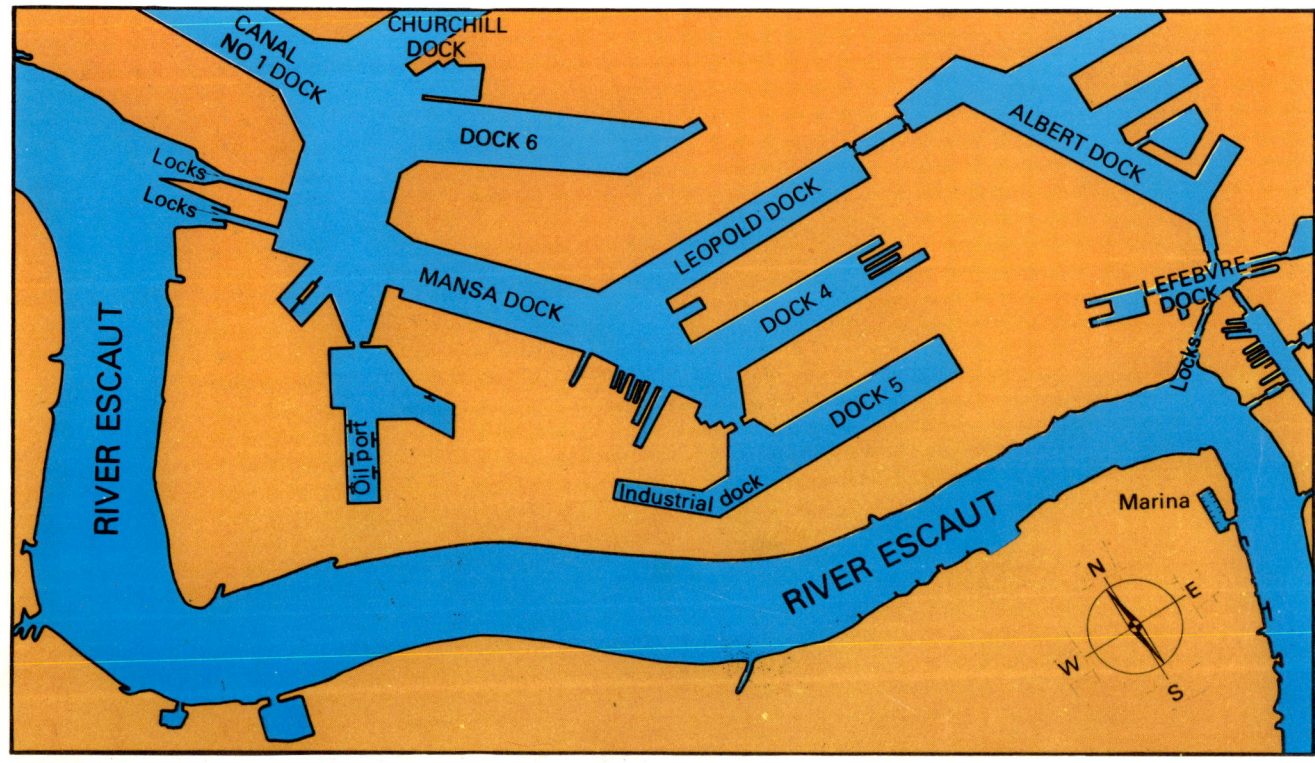

This is the world's greatest commercial port. A total of 232 million tonnes of goods are handled there annually. The new "Europort", which is being built at the mouth of the River Maas, will be the largest port in the world. It will be equipped with the most modern installations for dealing with every kind of cargo and will be able to receive vessels of up to 300,000 tonnes.

The key to the importance of the port of Hamburg is its situation on the left bank of the Elbe at a northern point of the mainland of Europe. In addition, it is situated beside a network of railways linking it to the whole of Germany and her neighbouring countries, and is linked to the Rhine, the Oder and the Baltic Sea by many canals.

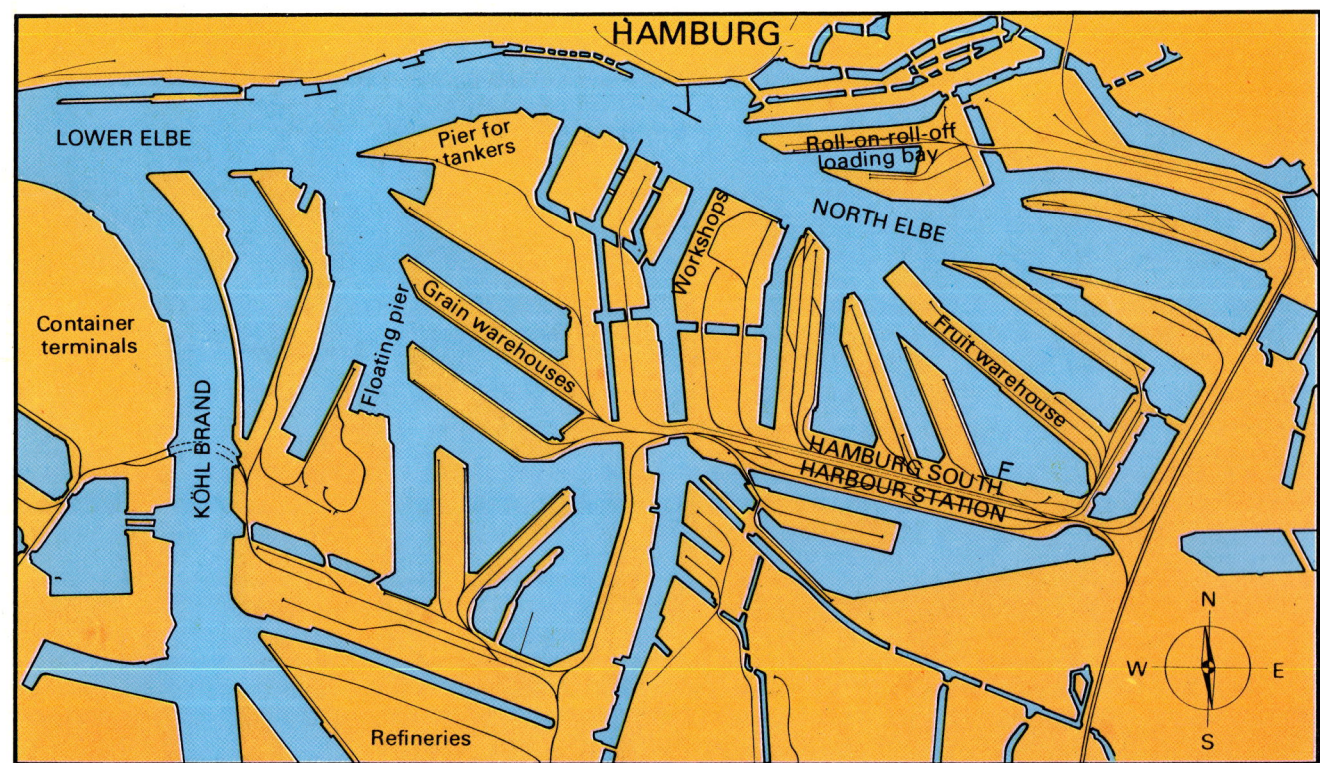

Plans to build industrial complexes of every kind in the port of Marseilles are turning it into not only the most important port in France but also one of the largest in the world. The reopening of the Suez Canal has played a major part in increasing its commercial importance and bringing its facilities for storage and the transport of raw materials into use again.

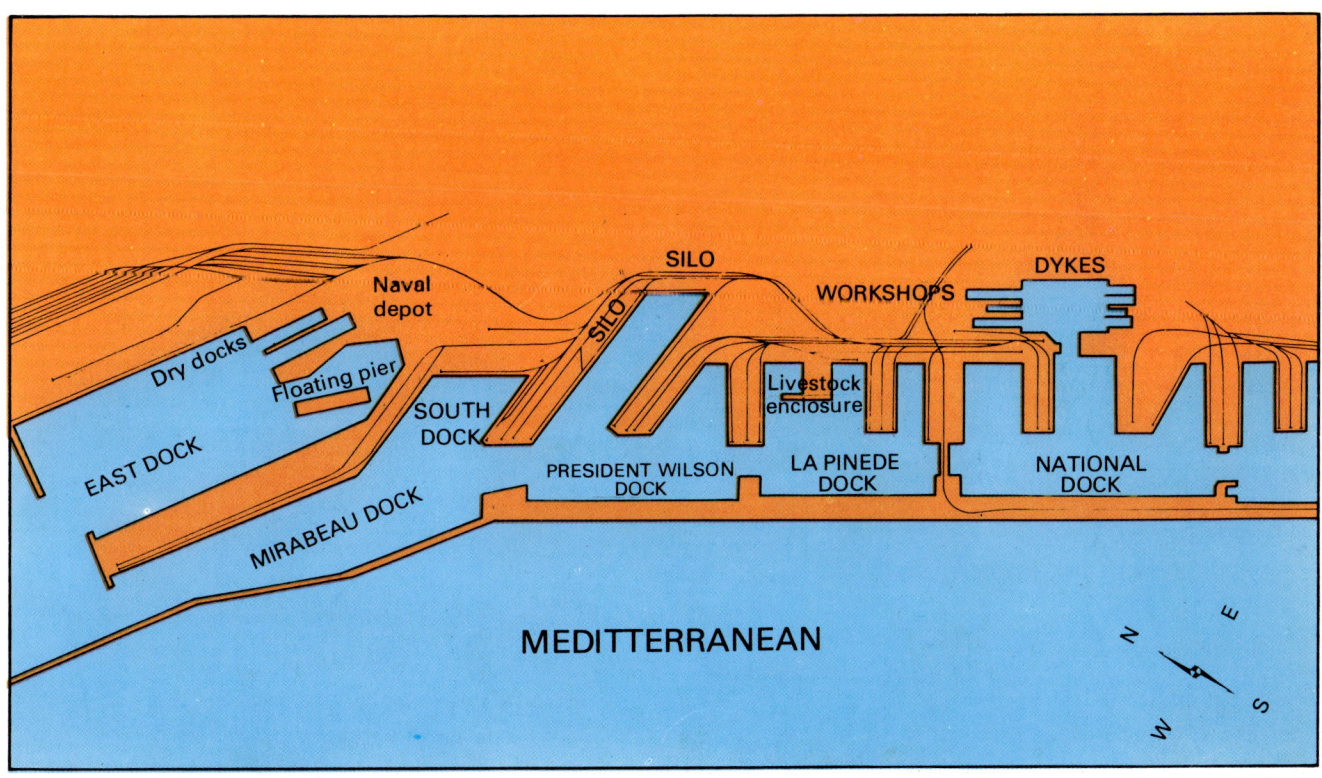

Glossary

BEACON. A signal indicating danger at sea or marking the direction of shipping lanes. They can be fixed or floating and may carry lights transmitting signals.

BEAM. The width of a boat, measured across the upper deck.

BOATSWAIN. The person in charge of the crew who oversees the work done on board. His duties include looking after the ship, seeing to supplies, keeping order and assigning work to the sailors. He may also sometimes act as captain or navigator.

BREAKWATER. A wall stretching out into the sea to protect a harbour or bay by breaking the force of waves.

BRIDGE. The place from which the captain steers the ship.

BUOY. A floating object fixed to the sea-bed by anchors. It marks a dangerous spot, a wreck or the entrance or exit of a harbour. It may be luminous or work by means of a whistle, a bell, a light and a bell, or a light and a whistle.

DISPLACEMENT. The volume of water drawn by a vessel and whose weight is equal to the weight of the vessel.

DRAUGHT. The depth of water a ship needs to float her.

FITTER-OUT. Someone who equips a vessel — i.e., provides it with everything it needs for sailing.

FOGHORN. A signal audible at long distances and used by ships to announce their presence in fog, their entry into or exit from a harbour, or to greet another ship, etc.

HAWSER. A rope which is thrown from the ship to the quay and tied to a mooring post; also the name for other ropes used in sailing.

HELMSMAN. The person who works the rudder of the ship to steer it.

HOLD. The inside of a ship between the lower deck and the keel. This is usually where the cargo is stowed.

HULL. The main "body" of the ship.

INLET. A narrow channel acting as the entrance to a harbour.

INNER HARBOUR. The most sheltered part of the port; used for loading and unloading ships under the easiest conditions of wind and weather. It may be natural or man-made. A large port has several harbours.

LENGTH. The length of a ship measured on deck from poop to prow.

MOORING POST. A post set into the edge of the quay and used for tying ships' hawsers to. It stands about 50cm high.

ORLOP. One of the floors of a ship where the crew's quarters are laid out.

PIER. A groyne or breakwater stretching out into the sea, built to protect the coast against waves; also at seaside holiday resorts it is used as a promenade and for entertainments.

PILOT. A skilled navigator with a detailed knowledge of certain waters and who steers vessels by eye; called coast or harbour pilot according to the location of operations.

POOP. The after-part or stern of a ship.

PORT. The left side of a vessel when looking towards the bow.

PROW. The front part of a ship.

RADAR. A device for detecting the position of an unseen object by means of electric beams bouncing off the object and registering on a screen.

RUDDER. A broad, flat piece hinged vertically to the poop of a vessel and used for steering it to port or starboard.

STARBOARD. The right side of a ship looking towards the bow.

STEVEDORE. The person in charge of stowing the cargo in the hold correctly so that the ship will not list (lean over).

TO BERTH. A ship berths when it comes up alongside the quay.

TO GO AGROUND. A ship goes aground when her hull touches a stony or sandy bottom and she is brought to a halt.

TO LIST. A ship lists when she leans to one side because of strong winds or badly positioned cargo.

TO SET SAIL. To unfurl a flag or sails and move out of the harbour towards the open sea.

TO VEER. To alter a ship's direction.

TO WEIGH ANCHOR. To raise the anchor so that the ship can move off.

TUG. A boat used for towing vessels by means of a cable, chain, etc.